Reflections on Narrative Practice:
Essays and interviews

Reflections on Narrative Practice:

Essays and interviews

by

Michael White

DULWICH CENTRE PUBLICATIONS
ADELAIDE SOUTH AUSTRALIA

Copyright © 2000 *by* **Dulwich Centre Publications**
ISBN 0 9577429 1 3

published by
Dulwich Centre Publications
Hutt St PO Box 7192
Adelaide, South Australia 5000
phone (61-8) 8223 3966 fax (61-8) 8232 4441
email: dcp@senet.com.au
www.dulwichcentre.com.au

The views expressed in this book are not necessarily those of the Publisher.

No part of this book may be reproduced or transmitted by any process whatsoever without the prior written permission of the Publisher.

Printed & manufactured in Australia by:
Graphic Print Group, Richmond, South Australia

100% recycled paper

Contents

Introduction		vii
Essays		
1.	Children, children's culture, and therapy	3
2.	Challenging the culture of consumption: Rites of passage and communities of acknowledgement	25
3.	Re-engaging with history: The absent but implicit	35
4.	Reflecting-team work as definitional ceremony revisited	59
Interviews		
5.	Diversity and family therapy	89
6.	Direction and discovery: A conversation about power and politics in narrative therapy	97
7.	Then and now ...	117
8.	On ethics and the spiritualities of the surface	129
9.	An exploration of aesthetics	161

Introduction

This collection of essays and interviews provide reflections on various aspects of narrative therapy: on the development of particular therapeutic practices; on the employment of key metaphors; on the possibilities that are shaped by poststructuralist thought; on the context of narrative therapy, including its location in the field of family therapies; on the relevance of these considerations to religious and spiritual notions; and more. It is my understanding that many of these reflections are topical, and it is my hope that they will contribute to the spirit of inquiry that is shaping contemporary developments in therapeutic practice.

There are many people to thank. Cheryl White for encouraging me to put this collection together in the first place. David Denborough for his enthusiasm for this project, for his helpful advice, for lending an editorial hand, and for being ever willing to take up whatever was left that needed to be done in the preparation of this book for publication. Jane Hales for taking on the layout of this book in her usual intrepid way, finding the necessary time in her already busy schedule, and not giving a second thought to the conditions brought on by the sweltering heat of high summer in Adelaide. And Ula Horwitz for providing some much appreciated assistance at the eleventh hour by doing a final proofread of the text.

A substantial section of this book is comprised of interviews. This section would not exist without the thoughtful interest of the people who instigated these interviews/conversations. Thanks to: Gene Combs, Jill Freedman, Myrna Gower, Michael Hoyt, Dave Spellman, and Jeff Zimmerman.

Michael White
January 2000

Essays

1.

Children, children's culture, and therapy

I have particularly appreciated this opportunity to write on the subject of children, children's culture, and therapy. This is because it provides me with occasion to put together an account of the contribution of children to the many therapeutic adventures that have been a source of joy to my life, and to the development of a range of therapeutic practices. A good part of what I know as narrative therapy has its roots in consultations with young children and their families.

Externalising conversations

Explorations of externalising conversations have for a long time been a feature of my work.[1] I have taken these explorations into my work with people who have sought consultations over a wide range of problems and concerns, from those of a relatively mild and short-term nature through to those that are often considered to be 'chronic' and 'psychiatric'.[2] When soliciting feedback from these people about their experience of our time together, very often it is the engagement with externalising conversations that is identified as a turning point for them in their efforts to satisfactorily address their problems and concerns. Amongst other things, externalising conversations have made it possible for people to separate their sense of identity from problem-saturated or deficit-centred accounts of who they are, and this has provided a basis for them to join with others in the rich description of alternative accounts of their lives, of their relationships, and of their identities.

As I reflect on the paragraph that I have just written, and on my experience of externalising conversations over the past couple of decades, I recognise that I remain fascinated with how these conversations open doors for the people who consult me. At this very moment I am thinking of a family that I met with this afternoon – a family short on resources and space, and one comprised of a mother and her first cousin, and four adult and near adult children. These children had, for some considerable time, been at loggerheads with each other over how they could manage to live in the same household and at the same time give expression to their contrasting and, on occasions, conflicting lifestyles and interests. Things didn't go at all well in the first fifteen or twenty minutes of our meeting. This was a painful time for us all. The tension rose as each party traded claims and counterclaims about various events, and voiced his/her conclusions about what this all said about each other's negative motives and intentions. In this way they were digging a big hole for each other, and, in the process of doing so, all scrabbling wildly to resist being pulled into it.

At last I found a space to ask these family members some questions about what their dissatisfactions reflected about how they would prefer things to be in their relationships with each other, and about what these preferences reflected about their values and beliefs. The responses to these questions paved the way for us to enter into conversations that were identifying of the forces at play that were derailing of family members in their efforts to live well together, and that were taking them all away from their preferred ways of being in life. I asked about what name might be given to these forces, and these were quickly identified as 'negative habits of thought and behaviour'. We were soon mapping out the effects of these habits of thought and behaviour through various dimensions of their lives and the relationships. Suddenly, in the course of this, the grown children of this family found themselves giving voice to alternative understandings of each other's actions and intentions, understandings that contradicted the earlier stated ones that had so negatively connoted these actions and intentions. In response to my request that family members reflect on the nature of these alternative understandings, they were characterised as 'touching' and 'compassionate'.

It was these alternative understandings that subsequently opened the door to the exploration of new possibilities for action for each family member, possibilities for action that might bring what was happening in this household more into line with how everyone wanted things to be in their relationships with each other. We were all warmed by this turn of events. And what a ride we'd had together over the course of our conversation! To go, via an externalising conversation, from such powerfully negative identity conclusions to an opening space conversation in such a relatively brief period of time was nothing short of uplifting.

Why this brief review of externalising conversations, and why include this story in a chapter about consulting with children and their families? Because it was with children that I first engaged in systematic explorations of externalising conversations, and because these shared explorations were so generative of ideas that I subsequently took them into my consultations with adolescents and adults. It was children's responses to these early efforts that so powerfully reinforced further developments in them: children's easy fit with these ways of speaking about the events of their lives; their unbridled enthusiasm for the new possibilities for action that these conversations presented; their sheer delight in entering into these more imaginative ways of speaking about what were so often considered to be deadly serious problems; and their joy in stepping into these conversations in ways that defied many a prediction about their continuing inability or powerlessness to address this predicament or that. The development of externalising conversations is very considerably a testimony to the contribution of the voices of many children.

Therapeutic documents

People often experience a rather tenuous hold on the sparkling events (often referred to as 'unique outcomes' or 'exceptions') of their lives that are identified in the course of therapeutic conversations. When this is the case, the life-changing options that become available through the identification and exploration of these events can be lost. These sparkling events are those that contradict the problem-saturated stories of people's lives, and the deficit-centred accounts of their identities. When taken into the story-lines of people's lives, these events contribute to the thickening of the alternative or counter-plots of their lives, and provide the foundations of new possibilities for action in relation to addressing the concerns and problems for which they seek therapy.

Practices of the written word, which have for a long time been a theme of narrative therapy, contribute significantly to the visibility, substantiation, and endurance of the sparkling events that are identified in narrative conversations – these practices of the written word document the more sparkling events of people's lives and in so doing contribute to 'rescuing the said from the saying of it', the 'told from the telling of it'. This documentation can take many forms, including certificates, letters, announcements, position statements, verse, song, and transcripts of therapeutic conversations.

As with externalising conversations, it was with children that David Epston and I first explored the use of therapeutic documents.[3] Children's responses to these explorations were not just powerfully reinforcing of a commitment to further develop different forms of therapeutic documents, but also contributed significantly to an appreciation of what are the significant and finer contours of these. In this way, children's responses have made a substantial contribution to the moulding of subsequent practices of the written word that I have taken into my consultations not just with other children, but also into my consultations with young people and adults who are living their lives out in a broad range of contexts.

Definitional ceremony

Narrative therapy engages with the idea that the establishment of identity is both a project and an achievement that takes place in the social domain, not a manifestation of specific properties of individuals that are given in particular accounts of 'human nature', or something that evolves according to the rules of whatever it is that this 'human nature' is taken to be. According to this notion of identity, the development of a sense of personal authenticity is the outcome of social processes in which specific claims about one's identity – claims that are socially negotiated – are acknowledged or 'verified' by others. It is understood that it is this acknowledgement and verification that is authenticating of people's identity claims – this acknowledgement and verification contributes to a sense of being 'at one' with whatever the identity claims happen to be.

This account of identity is reflected in the commonly experienced phenomenon of multiple authenticities. Some examples: people at times find themselves in two minds over which course of action might suit them, even when the options under consideration directly contradict each other; it is not unusual for people to engage in an action that they later characterise as an 'It just wasn't me' type expression, even though at the time there seemed a certain logic or even inevitability to this action; on certain occasions people become aware of a lack of coherence in their views or opinions about matters, even those over which they feel strongly about, and secretly acknowledge to themselves that they are not quite as 'together' as they appear to the world.

The phenomenon of multiple authenticities is an outcome of the fact that people live out their lives in various contexts or zones (for example, in different relational and institutional contexts of home, work, school, play and so on) in which different identity claims are verified. It is through this social process of verification that people come to experience being at one with the identity claims that are negotiated in these different contexts or zones of life. However, despite this common experience of multiple authenticities, some authenticities are more keenly experienced and more constituting or shaping of people's lives than others. On account of the hegemony of some of the verifying social forces that are active in the primary zones of people's lives, social forces that are shaping of people's dominant identity claims, many of the authenticities that contradict a person's sense of 'at oneness' with these dominant identity claims of their life are rather fleetingly experienced. In these circumstances, dominant identity claims can become relatively unshakeable identity conclusions.

Many of the practices of narrative therapy assist people to break from the identity claims that are associated with the problem-saturated accounts of their lives, and from the authenticities that are the outcome of the social verification of these identity claims, which have become the dominant ones. These practices of narrative therapy also provide a basis for the identification and/or generation of alternative and 'preferred' identity claims. Once established, other narrative practices contribute to the authentication of these alternative and preferred identity claims. These practices introduce processes of acknowledgement that are verifying of these preferred identity claims; processes of acknowledgement that are richly describing of these claims, and that contribute to people's sense of being 'at one' with these claims; processes of acknowledgement that are generative of alternative experiences of authenticity.

These practices of acknowledgement invariably engage an audience of outsider-witnesses in the retelling of the stories that are associated with people's alternative identity claims, retellings that extend on the boundaries of the original tellings, retellings in which the stories of people's lives become joined around shared themes, purposes, values and, at times, commitments. These tellings and retellings can be understood to compose an informal 'regrading' definitional ceremony, and the people whose lives are at the centre of these retellings invariably find this transporting of them.

As with the development of many other narrative practices, it was in my consultations with children that I first explored the contribution of the audience or the outsider-witness group to the authentication of the alternative and preferred identity claims that are routinely derived in narrative conversations. It was in this work with children that I became conscious of the extent to which it is the therapist's business to arrange therapy as a context for ceremonies of redefinition – to arrange social arenas in which there are opportunities for people to step into alternative and preferred identity claims and to perform them, and in which these claims can be acknowledged by an appropriate audience. It was during my earlier consultations with families that children so powerfully reinforced my interest in the definitional ceremony metaphor. Invariably I found these children to be highly enthusiastic about opportunities to engage more fully with the alternative and more positive identity claims that were derived in our conversations. Conversely, in all of these consultations, children always made it clear that they were decidedly unenthusiastic about being subject to yet more of the familiar detective-style inquiry into their alternative 'Yes, I really do want to change this about my life' identity claims – detective-style inquiry that shapes questions like: 'I don't think you really mean that. Aren't you saying this because this is just what you want us to hear?'.

It was children's responses to these explorations of the definitional ceremony metaphor that freed me from any illusion that I might have had that social processes of authentication are relatively peripheral to the therapeutic endeavour, and perhaps just something to be tacked on as an afterthought. This prompted me to more fully engage with this metaphor in the structuring of a range of therapeutic practices that I have taken not just into my consultations with other children, but into my meetings with young people and adults seeking consultation over a broad range of concerns and issues.

Meaning-making

A primary focus of narrative therapy is people's expressions of their experiences of life. The conversations of this therapy are shaped by the proposal that, in order for people to express their experiences of the worlds that they live through, they must engage in acts of the interpretation of these experiences. Not only do these interpretive acts make it possible for people to give meaning to their experiences of the world, rendering life sensible to themselves and to others, but these acts also shape their expression of this lived experience. According to this understanding, people's expressions of life, which are actually shaping or constitutive of their lives, are units of meaning and experience, and these elements are inseparable.

The conversations of narrative therapy are not premised on the idea that the meanings that people construct in these acts of interpretation are radically invented – these meanings are not independently derived from out of the blue or from inside people's heads as an outcome of unique thought, or out of some singular consciousness that provides for people an apprehension of the world 'as it is', whatever that world might be. Rather, this therapy is associated with the proposition that the meanings that people derive in these acts of interpretation are determined by the interpretive resources that are available to them, and further, that these meanings are negotiated in communities of people and within the various terms and institutions of culture. According to this understanding, meaning is at once a personal, relational, and cultural achievement.

The interpretive resource that is privileged in narrative conversations is the story. It is here assumed that the structure of narrative provides the principle frame of intelligibility for people in their day-to-day lives. It is through this frame that people negotiate meaning. It is through this frame that people make sense of their experiences of the events of their lives. It is through narrative structure that people are able to link together their experiences of the events of their lives in sequences that unfold through time according to specific themes. And it is assumed that it is this storying of experience that provides the basis for knowing action in the world.

These understandings and considerations of the processes and structures of meaning-making are significant in the shaping of narrative conversations with people who consult therapists. But why include here this brief review of these understandings and considerations? I do this because although there exist in the literature multiple sources of support for these understandings and considerations (take, for example, what has been written in the name of the 'anthropology of experience' [E. Bruner, 1986; J. Bruner, 1990]), it was in my consultations with young children that I was first able to extend on my appreciation of the significance of narrative structures in the derivation of meaning. It was in my consultations with children that I was able to gain a practical grasp of the extent to which the negotiation of meaning is both a significant personal and social achievement. And it was in these consultations that I was able to grasp the fuller implications of the specificity of these meanings in the shaping of, or in the embracing of, people's lives.

In children's lives, the negotiation of meaning is a highly visible achievement, one that is often hard-won. For young children there is so much about the world that is novel, so many new experiences to be negotiated, so many gaps to be filled in their understandings of life. Nowhere is recourse to narrative structures in achieving all of this more manifestly apparent than it is in children's efforts to understand their experiences of life. Nowhere are the social processes of the negotiation of meaning more conspicuous than in children's culture. And it is in children's acts of living that the life-shaping implications of particular meanings is so evident.

On this account, my consultations with children have been powerfully influential in the shaping of my practice. These consultations have contributed to learnings that have assisted me to join with other children, adolescents, and adults in finding windows of opportunity for a re-engagement in the processes of meaning-making and identity formation – even for those who have believed that matters of their own identity were forever sealed, forever set in cement.

Childhood and children's culture

As I wrote the above paragraphs about what I understand to be children's contributions to elements of my practice, my mind kept filling with many other thoughts about their contributions to yet other elements of my practice. On account of this, I found the decision to change direction at this point in this paper to be a difficult one. But it was important to me to include some reflections on why it might be that children's ways of life have made such a contribution to the development of practices that have provided, for others who stand in the culture of young people and the culture of adults, what seem to be novel but effective ways of going about addressing the predicaments of their lives. And it was also important for me to address the sort of conclusions that evoke the 'nature' of children as an explanation for this, for, in this acknowledgement of the contribution of children to the development of these practices, it has not been my intention to contribute to further to naturalistic explanations of this sort.

I am sure that you, the reader, will have a familiarity with the sort of explanations that I am referring to. There are many popular narratives that construct children's expressions as manifestations of human nature. In fact, according to the greater proportion of these popular narratives, childhood is a state of being in the context of human development that is closest to nature. For example, take those narratives that are highly venerating of childhood. According to these narratives, not only are children's expressions more in accord with human nature than are the expressions of adults generally, but, it is said, because children's understandings are less sullied by the forces of socialisation, they have a truer consciousness of the world as it really is. Further, these accounts assert that, because people in these early stages of life are less repressed than people in other stages of life, children are more real and more honest in their expressions of life. The high value that some of these narratives place on childhood is reflected in the extent to which childhood is exoticised – it is proposed that in children's voices can be found a true and innate wisdom that adults are usually bereft of, and would be well advised to reclaim. These narratives stimulate the numerous developments in the fields of psychotherapy and popular psychology that aim to assist people to find guidance in addressing the predicaments of their lives through a reclaiming of their childhood. According to these narratives that are venerating of childhood, childhood is synonymous with originality.

Not all narratives that construct children's expressions as a manifestation of human nature are venerating of childhood. For example, there are those popular narratives that construct children's nature to be unruly and uncivilised, and in need of very considerable guidance, training, and even taming, without which, it is understood, children will grow up to become antisocial, impulsive and disinhibited adults. According to these narratives, rather than children having a truer consciousness of the world as it really is, their understandings of life are often classed as creative and cute, but naive. Rather than expressing a true wisdom, the thinking of young minds, it is said, is marred by faulty and inaccurate cognitions, and features and inability to grasp the facts of life in the way that more disciplined and mature minds are able to. In these narratives, childhood is synonymous not with originality, but with immaturity.

In characterising here two groups of popular narratives that construct children's expressions as manifestations of human nature, I wish to acknowledge that there are many other popular narratives that do the same but that don't fit within either of these characterisations, and, as well, yet other narratives that manage to combine elements of the these two groups. Also, in characterising these narratives in the way that I have, it has not been my intention to criticise them or to evaluate their relative merits. It is my understanding that such narratives of human development are influential in the shaping of lives of young people, of their relationships with others, and of their very identities. In this way, these narratives are associated with a range of consequences for how people life their lives, consequences among which include certain possibilities, but also limitations and potential hazards. Although I have described 'popular' narratives here, I haven't employed this adjective in order to lowly rank these narratives in relation to the narratives of human development of the professional disciplines. I believe that the narratives of human development of the professional disciplines are informed by, and, in turn, are shaping of, these popular narratives.

If we do not take recourse to popular narratives about children's nature in our efforts to understand why it might be that children's ways of life have made such a contribution to therapeutic practices of the sort that I described at the outset of this paper, what options are left for us to accomplish such an understanding. Another approach to this question is to consider these contributions within the context of culture and history. This approach would be one that would seek to provide an account of the ways in which children's expressions are shaped by the culture of childhood. According to this approach, children's ways of life would be understood to be as much a product of children's culture as the ways of adults can be understood to be a product of adult culture.

Children's culture, as a general phenomenon, is a relatively recent development in western culture. Although the history of this culture can be traced over many centuries, until approximately two hundred years ago childhood was a category of life only available in those families of the very privileged. For the very great majority, childhood began at the end of the eighteenth century and the beginning of the nineteenth century. Until this time, young and relatively short people were subject to much the same forces and conditions of life as were older and taller people. Since its inception as a more general phenomenon, childhood has had profound effects in shaping the lives of young and relatively short people. These effects are generally considered to be positive, and the protection of young people is usually cited as one of the foremost achievements of this development. For example, associated with the rise of childhood, and providing considerable impetus to this, was the development and introduction of legislation, in England (and simultaneously in Australia) in the 1820s and 1830s, designed to protect young people from exploitation in the work force.

Over its two hundred year history as a general phenomenon, there have been many contributions from many quarters to the development of children's culture. Like any culture, children's culture is not static. It is a negotiated culture that is constantly being shaped and reshaped according the manufacture of a range of narratives about children's nature, according to expert claims and counterclaims about what is in young people's best interest and what is not, through the ongoing production of developmental theories, by the varying persuasions of different educationalists, by the story books and novels of the authors of children's literature, and, of course, by young people's engagement with and mediation of all these constituting influences as they go about living their lives. Although many of these constituting elements sponsor shared understandings about childhood, there is also a significant degree of contestation between different elements, and they are not all equal in terms of influence. For example, the story tellers and novelists of children's literature have a particularly elevated status, and many of these make contributions to children's culture through counter-narratives that are subverting of many of the taken-for-granted ideas about the lives and the identities of young people. An example of books written in this vein are Astrid Lindgren's *Pippy Longstockings*, *Brothers Lionheart*, and *The Robber's Daughter*.

To understand children's expressions of life to be cultural and historical phenomena provides an opportunity for us to consider a range of questions that I believe to be highly relevant to our work with children – questions like: What were the historical conditions that gave rise to the notion of the category of childhood?; What are the modes of life and thought that are associated with this category?; What were the conditions that contributed to this notion coming to centre stage and informing the development of this as a general social phenomenon?; In what ways has this notion been taken up, and to what use has it been put?; What are the continuities and the discontinuities in the history of this development?; How might we know the intended consequences of this development, and how might we trace the unintended consequences of this?; What are the modes of life and thought that are associated with this category of human life?; What did the development and introduction of this category make possible?; How might the limitations and hazards of this development be made visible? And so on.

It is not my intention to address this range of questions here in this essay. I will restrict my attention to a brief discussion of what I believe to be some of the limitations and hazards associated with the development of a culture of childhood, and then discuss what I understand to be some of the possibilities that accompany this development.

Limitations and hazards of childhood

Although there can be cited many developments of the past two hundred years that provide ample support for claims about the benefits of childhood, and for celebrating this achievement, it has become increasingly apparent in recent decades that childhood has significant shortcomings. For the young people of children's culture are subject to abuse at alarming rates, and young people who have the status of children appear, on account of this status, to have little, if any, legitimate voice on this abuse and on a range of other matters that directly concern their lives.

In many contexts of contemporary life, to invite children into conversations in which they are radically consulted about their own lives is the exception to the rule. There is now such an abundance of explanations about children's expressions of life, such an avalanche of competing 'truths' about the origins of such expressions, such a multiplicity of assertions about children's nature and about their needs, and such an explosion of narratives about child development and its stages, that it now appears that childhood has been theorised in all of its intimate particularities. Regardless of the relative merits and veracity of these theories, they are routinely taken up, in popular and in professional culture, in the interpretation of, and in the management of, children's actions in ways that neglect any exploration of the possibilities that are available for consulting children about these actions. In fact, in relation to children's expressions of life, the term action is rarely employed. It is another term, child 'behaviour', that is taken up in describing these expressions. This is a structuralist rendering of action, and I will provide a brief account of this here.

When structuralist understandings are applied to people's expressions of living and of identity, the metaphors of depth and surface, inner and outer, and centre and periphery, are invariably employed and contrasted. In contrasting these metaphors, structuralist understandings recast action as 'behaviour' that is a surface manifestation of the elements or essences that have a deep residence in people's lives. People's expressions of living and of identity are considered to be surface manifestations of certain elements or essences or forces – like needs, personal properties, characteristics, attributes, impulses, drives, motives, desires, assets, and so on – or disorders of these elements, essences and forces. According to these understandings, these elements, essences and forces are located at some depth in people's lives, and in particular sites at the centre of the self – for example within people's psyche, at their emotional centre, or whatever.

Structuralist understandings of human action are pervasive in contemporary western culture. It is now widely believed – in fact, it is largely taken for granted – that there is such a thing as a 'self' that is the bedrock of, and at the centre of, human identity and action, despite the fact that this is a recent idea, and one that is relatively novel in the history of the world's cultures. And it is now generally accepted that there are such things as elements, essences and forces that reside that the centre of a self, and that though a structuralist analysis of the 'surface manifestations' of these elements, essences and forces, the 'truth' of acts of living can be revealed.

When it comes to expressions of people's lives that are considered problematic in this context or that, structuralist understandings represent these expressions as surface manifestations of a distortion of, or a disorder in, the elements or essences or forces that reside at the centre of the self. These understandings of life contribute to the generation of many theories about human behaviour, and these theories inform the development of systems of analyses that can be placed over people's lives. It is commonly accepted that these systems of analyses make possible the translation and the interpretation of the expressions of the 'surface' of life. These interpretations are understood to be identifying of and classifying of the disorders of the elements and essences that give rise to the expressions of living that are in question.

When the expressions of children's lives are the subject of structuralist understandings, these expressions are taken into systems of analyses and assessment that provide for the translation and interpretation of them as 'behaviours'.[4] In the course of this, children's lives can become the focus of 'assessment', 'management', 'intervention', and/or 'treatment' in a power relationship that is marginalising of, and frequently disqualifying of, the knowledges and skills of living that have been generated through the history of their engagement with the world. This is a power relationship in which others know more about the predicaments that children experience than children themselves know about these predicaments, and in which the relevant solutions to these predicaments are to be found in domains of knowledge that are distant from children's immediate experiences of life and from children's culture.

Although it is not just children that have become the subject of the structuralist understandings and practices that I describe here, children's expressions have, for some considerable time, been at the centre of modern structuralist inquiry. In few contexts are they accorded a voice on the sort of alternative understandings of their expressions that invoke notions like conscious purpose and intention, considered choice, cherished beliefs, personal values, nourished wishes, and preferred hopes. I don't believe that it is necessary for me to here draw out more fully the consequences of the application of structuralist understandings of action as behaviour when these understandings are taken into the sort of power relations that I have described, except to say that it is little wonder that so many young people wish to speed their exit from childhood.

Possibilities of childhood

Despite the apparent limitations and hazards that are associated with the development of a culture of childhood, this development has also brought with it certain possibilities. This culture, which has been shaped by the ideas, interests and investments of so many parties and institutions of our modern world, and by young people's creative engagement with these ideas, interests, and investments, provides an opportunity for young people to engage with some modes of life and thought that are outside of the routine habits of thought and action of adult culture. For example, because play in various senses, including in the sense of 'as if', is so positively valued in children's culture, young people have the opportunity to bring together many things, including words and ideas, that are not routinely brought together in the wider culture. Such achievements can have the effect of unsettling what are regarded to be the settled certainties of the world, and in this way young people's expressions often provide a source of the novel in ways that can contribute significantly to the regeneration of the wider culture.

Such achievements have certainly had a significant effect on my work. In my consultations with families, I can think of many occasions upon which children's expressions have encouraged me to think past what I would have otherwise thought, to inquire about things that I would not otherwise have inquired about, and to question ideas and actions that I take for granted and that I would not otherwise have questioned. I know that these experiences have contributed to developments that have been carried forward into my work not just with other children, but also with other young people and adults.

Some of the possibilities that are available to young people that are associated with the development of childhood relate to what might be considered to be 'exemptions' from some of the dominant requirements for the shaping of personhood in general culture. (There is, however, a price to be paid for this exemption. For the understandings of life that young people develop as an outcome of this are often taken to be 'childlike', and lowly ranked.) I am here referring to the requirements of self-possession, self-containment and coherence in the development of the single-voiced and encapsulated identities that are venerated in contemporary mainstream culture. On account of these exemptions, the young people of children's culture have the opportunity of exploring multiple senses of self, and do not experience the social sanctions in response to multi-voiced expressions of life that adults experience. But more than this – these multi-voiced expressions are often powerfully reinforced. For example, consider the fact that the imaginary or invisible friends of childhood are not just tolerated in many families, but welcomed and even consulted about matters of concern to the young person's life.

In many of my consultations with families I have been made aware of many of the benefits of children's performance of multi-voiced identities. These benefits include the generation of a greater range of ideas about how to go about addressing the various predicaments that are of concern to the members of these families, and, on account of the fact that these young people are not so powerfully tied to particular accounts of their identity, the greater freedom that is available for them to take up these ideas. Through the witnessing of the benefits of this exemption I have found considerable support for the development of therapeutic practices that assist other young people and adults to break from single-voiced senses of their identities, and to re-member their lives in ways that provide them with a range of possibilities for action in the world that would not otherwise be available to them (White 1997).

Another significant exemption that it available to the young people of children's culture is one that makes it possible for them to have a range of connections with other young people that are valued, and that don't fit with the narrow range of relational forms of contemporary western culture that are assigned merit or worth. The word friendship is insufficient to describe the broad range of liaisons, alliances and coalitions that young people of children's culture enter into and highly value, and being privy to the significance of these connections through my consultations has encouraged me to redouble my efforts to assist other young people and adults to find a way of describing and to more positively value many of the connections of their lives that don't reproduce those favoured relational forms of mainstream culture.

In this section of this paper I have described just some of the possibilities that have become available to young people through the development of children's culture. Although there are many other possibilities that could be described here, it is not my intention to do this at the present time. However, I do want to share a couple of reflections on what I have just written about these possibilities. These reflections take me back to some of the acknowledgements of the first pages of this paper. I am thinking of the connection between children's explorations of multi-voiced senses of self, and their externalisation of some of these senses as separate identities that are out in the world – for example, in the development of imaginary friends – and the development of externalising conversations as a therapeutic practice relevant to other young people and adults, as well as to children.

I have also again been thinking about the therapeutic practices that are shaped by the definitional ceremony metaphor, and reflecting on the extent to which my consultations with children have been confirming of an account of authenticity that challenges structuralist or essentialist accounts of this; that is, challenging of the idea that there is an authenticity to be discovered that is the bedrock of identity, the discovery of which is essential to people becoming who they really are. This challenge to structuralist or essentialist accounts of life is apparent in children's readiness and capacity to be other than who they are, in their habit of bringing together things that are not usually brought together to produce yet something else, in their comfort with multi-voiced identities, and in the significance that they accord their connections with other children in matters of self-definition.

Further considerations

In an earlier section of this paper, I proposed the option of stepping back from the structuralist understandings of life and the narratives of children's nature, and suggested that there might be much to be gained by understanding childhood to be a historical and cultural product. In making this proposal, it wasn't my intention to argue the relative merits and veracity of these narratives, and of the developmental theories associated with them. I have endeavoured to support this proposal by providing an account of just some of the considerations of children's expressions that become available when conceiving of childhood as a cultural and historical product, and will conclude this paper with yet other considerations that have been significant to me in shaping my work with children and their families.

Contribution to parenting

The first of these considerations has to do with children's contribution to parenting, and the importance of this being explicitly acknowledged in therapeutic contexts. I believe that stepping back from theories of children's behaviour and development has made it more possible for me to be aware of and to acknowledge the contribution that they make to the development of the more empathic and compassionate parenting practices of their parents, and the extent to which they collaborate with their parents in the expression of these practices. In this usually hidden parent-child partnership, children's responses to their parents' expressions of parenting significantly shape these expressions – these expressions are co-generated in the context of this partnership.

As well, when children have the opportunity, they not only give feedback about which of the number of available and already established options for parental action are the preferred ones in given situations, but also find ways of reinforcing preferred parental actions that are the outcome of chance events or happenstance. And there are those occasions upon which children directly advise parents about options for parental action that they would not have otherwise thought of.

Apart from this, there are times when children give their parents notice that certain parenting actions are unacceptable. This is accomplished in various ways, through non-verbal acts of resistance and direct statements that some actions are just not okay, to some of the more sophisticated strategies that many children are familiar with, and that are circulated widely in children's culture. How many parents have been pulled up short by disapproving children by utterances like: 'How could you, my very own father, have said such a thing?', 'Who would ever have believed a child's mother could do this?', 'Who would have thought this of you?'.

In making these observations about children's contributions to parenting practices, I am aware of the significance of the power imbalance in the parent/child relationship. I am also aware that the magnitude of this imbalance varies significantly from one relationship to the next, from one household to the next, and from one wider context to the next. Some parents use their position of authority to abuse and to exploit their children, and some others who do not explicitly do this nonetheless establish the parent/child relationship as a virtual state of domination for the child. Because of this variation, some children have the opportunity of making a far more significant contribution to parenting practices than other children. However, even in those situations where parents have used their position of authority to abuse and in other ways exploit their children, and even in those situations in which parents have established these virtual states of domination, I invariably find that children have found effective ways of modifying some of the actions of their parents despite the risks associated with doing so. Apart from instituting steps to address these abuses of power, on these occasions it has been particularly important to join with the children concerned in the identification of these initiatives that have been to a degree successful in modifying the actions of their parents.

Children's solution knowledges

The second of these considerations has to do with children's solution knowledges, and the importance of identifying these and richly describing them in the context of therapeutic conversations. Breaking from the narratives of human nature and from the associated developmental theories can open possibilities for children to be consulted about how their own solution knowledges might be applied to the events of their lives that are of a concern to their parents/caretakers. Children have a know-how that is relevant to the negotiation of many of the complexities that they face in the different contexts of their own lives. Some of this know-how is, of necessity, relatively sophisticated, because children do not often have access to the sort of power that would be required to simply make happen what they want to have happen – they rarely have the power available to them to achieve the ends that they desire through independent and singular action.

Unfortunately this know-how that children often have at their fingertips can easily be disregarded by parents and others who are concerned about the actions of these children. This often consigns parents to a lonely struggle with difficult dilemmas over the different courses of action that are available to them, and over the possible consequences of these different courses of action. And it leaves parents more vulnerable to 'losing it' when they have already tried many things to address the actions that are of concern to them, when they are particularly outraged about what their child has done, or when they are generally fatigued. In these circumstances children are not usually consulted about these dilemmas over what sort of parental action might be effective, about what consequences might be in the children's own best interests in the long run, or about aspects of the children's know-how that might be applicable to the situation. When these circumstances are present in families seeking therapy, this can be an ideal time for therapists to consult children in ways that make possible the exploration of their solution knowledges, and in ways that present options for them to take these up in addressing the concerns.

Children's nurturing

The third of these considerations has to do with children's nurturing skills, and the importance of the recognition and honouring of these in therapeutic contexts. Accounts of child-rearing practice that are informed by the developmental theories can render invisible, to therapists, the extent to which children are engaged in relations of reciprocity with their parents around expressions of tolerance, acceptance, patience, perseverance, caring and compassion. At times this reciprocity extends to the humouring of parents when things are getting a little out of hand for them, and to acts of benevolence that make it more possible for parents to deal with some of the difficult things that they are finding it hard to deal with. This benevolence is also evident in the way that children often ignore the occasions during which parents make embarrassments of themselves, and in the way that children contribute to the lessening of any humiliation that parents might experience at these times: 'It's okay. You are still my mother/father'. Theories of child development can also render invisible the extent to which, in children's culture, there is a great deal of mutual caring and support that takes place between children. This is particularly evident in communities where families are facing very considerable hardship.

Conclusion

I have provided an account of children's contributions to the development of some of the practices of narrative therapy. Understanding these contributions to be the outcome of young people's engagement with children's culture has the effect of considerably broadening therapeutic inquiry in all consultations with children and their families. In the context of this inquiry, therapy becomes an adventure that has the potential to take us beyond the known, and into delight.

Notes

1. White, 1984, 1986, 1988/89, 1989, 1991. See also Freedman & Combs, 1996; Freeman et al., 1997; Monk et al., 1997; Zimmerman & Dickerson, 1996.
2. See White, 1995.
3. See White & Epston, 1989.
4. This occurs in the contexts of children's everyday lives: in families, schools, hospitals, day-care and after-school care centres, sporting clubs, clinics, counselling centres, and so on.

References

Bruner, E. 1986: 'Ethnography as narrative.' In Turner, V. & Bruner, E. (eds), *The Anthropology of Experience*. Chicago: University of Illinois Press.

Bruner, J. 1990: *Acts of Meaning*. Cambridge, MA: Harvard University Press.

Freedman, J. & Combs, G. 1996: *Narrative Therapy: The social construction of preferred realities*. New York: Norton.

Freeman, J., Epston, D. & Lobovits, D. 1997: *Playful Approaches to Serious Problems: Narrative therapy with children and their families*. New York: Norton.

Monk, G., Winslade, J., Crocket, K. & Epston, D. 1997: *Narrative Therapy in Practice: The archaeology of hope*. San Francisco: Jossey-Bass.

White, M. 1984: 'Pseudo-encopresis: From avalanche to victory, from vicious to virtuous cycles.' *Family Systems Medicine*, 2(2).

White, M. 1986: 'Negative explanation, restraint and double description: A template for family therapy.' *Family Process*, 25(2).

White, M. 1988/89: 'The externalizing of the problem and the re-authoring of lives and relationships.' *Dulwich Centre Newsletter*, Summer.

White, M. & Epston, D. 1989: *Literate Means to Therapeutic Ends*. Adelaide: Dulwich Centre Publications. (Reprinted 1990 as *Narrative Means to Therapeutic Ends*. New York: Norton.)

White, M. 1991: 'Deconstruction and therapy.' *Dulwich Centre Newsletter*, No.2.

White, M. 1995: 'Psychotic experience and discourse.' In White, M., *Re-authoring Lives: Interviews and essays*. Adelaide: Dulwich Centre Publications. Interviewed by Ken Stewart.

White, M. 1997: *Narratives of Therapists' Lives*. Adelaide: Dulwich Centre Publications.

Zimmerman, J. & Dickerson, V. 1996: *If Problems Talked: Narrative therapy in action*. New York: Guilford Press.

2.

Challenging the culture of consumption:
Rites of passage and communities of acknowledgement[1]*

We routinely experience extraordinary encouragement to engage in the consumption of various substances in daily life, many of which are addictive. It could be said that contemporary culture is a 'culture of consumption'. There is an ever-increasing range of these substances available to us, the consumption of which is put to many different uses that are shaped by many different circumstances. For some persons, the quantity and/or the addictive nature of the substances they are consuming – whether they be legal, illicit or by prescription – becomes a problem to them and/or to others. When this is the case, these persons often find themselves consulting professional therapists.

In these consultations, persons are often oriented to questions like: 'Why can't I stop taking these drugs?' or 'Why can't I resist alcohol?' Confronted by questions such as these, therapists who have an appreciation of the extent to which ours is a culture of consumption are likely to suggest the exploration of other questions: 'Why is it that some persons don't take drugs?', 'Why is it that

---

* This paper was first published in 1997 in the Nos. 2 & 3 issue (special edition) of the *Dulwich Centre Newsletter*, entitled: 'New perspectives on addiction'.

some persons don't take more drugs than they do?', or 'Why is it that some persons don't consume excesses of alcohol?'. The exploration of questions like these gives emphasis to the many cultural forces that are inciting of an excessive consumption of a range of different substances. These questions, and others like 'How, under these circumstances, is it possible for you to have this desire to break your life from this substance?' or 'How, under these circumstances, have you been able to nurture this possibility of an alcohol free life?' also open possibilities for the exploration of some of the more sparkling facts of persons' lives that have been overshadowed and rendered invisible. And the exploration of these facts contributes to the development of accounts of the counter-plots of persons' lives – for example, of 'resistance to substance abuse', and of 'self-care'.

The emphasis given here to the cultural forces that are inciting of the consumption of substances is significant, for perhaps the most important first consideration for persons who want to change their relationship with a substance is to have an appreciation of what they will be up against in pursuing that ambition. If it is a person's conception that breaking from an addiction and/or the excessive consumption of substances is principally a matter of refusing pills, stepping back from the bottle, or disposing of the needles, they are very likely setting themselves up for an experience of humiliating failure that will be further complicating to their lives. With this conception, there is a high risk of their good intentions turning sour very rapidly. With this conception, a person will be unaware of what they are letting themselves in for in making such a decision, and will not have the opportunity to adequately prepare for their separation from addiction and/or the excessive consumption of substances.

It is not just the cultural forces that are inciting of the consumption of substances that persons are up against in their desire to change their relationship with substances. And it is not just throwing off the weight of the history and the traditions of the culture of consumption that is required. For most persons, changing one's relationship with substances requires a break from much of one's life as it is known. It is to break from a familiar sense of being in the world. It is to break from certain ways of relating to one's own life and to the lives of others. And, for many, it is to break from familiar networks of people.

Breaking from addictions and/or the excessive consumption of substances usually requires a very major life shift – something akin to a migration of identity, an act of intentionally leaving one's life behind in order to make a new life for oneself. Pursuing a desire to revise one's relationship with a substance sets a person on a journey, and leaving the territory of life that one has long inhabited is the first stage of this journey. This departure is not accompanied by simultaneous arrival in some other territory of life in which the person finds a place of their own. In departing from the known, a person does not step into another known. This departure is an exit into the unknown. Persons can only be certain of the general direction. But they will remain uncertain about how far they must travel, and what will become of them along the way.

A rite of passage

I often invoke the rite of passage metaphor when I'm consulted by persons who want to break from an addiction and/or from the excessive consumption of substances. Following van Gennep (1960) and Turner (1969), three stages to rites of passage can be discerned. First is the *separation phase,* at which a person breaks from their life as they know it. This marks the beginning of the journey. Second, there is the *liminal phase.* This is a 'betwixt and between' phase, in which one's familiar sense of being in the world is absent, and where nothing means quite what it did before. This phase is invariably characterised by periods of disorientation and confusion, and times of significant despair. Third, there is the *reincorporation phase.* Reincorporation is achieved when a person finds that they've arrived at another place in life, where they experience a 'fit' that provides for them a sense of once again being at home with themselves and with a way of life. At this time, persons regain a sense of being knowledged and skilled in matters of living.

Work that is informed by the rite of passage metaphor provides persons with a general map of the experiences that are to be expected in breaking from addiction and/or excessive consumption of substances. This map that emphasises the phases of separation, liminality, and reincorporation is often an invaluable aid to journeys that can be fraught. This map provides persons with a general guide through the territories that lie ahead. It provides persons with a basis for predicting the experiences that are to be had. It informs persons in the preparations that must be made ahead of departure. Without a map to assist persons in this way, there is a significantly greater risk that they will turn back before completing the journey.

Before taking a first step in this migration of identity, in the lead up to the separation phase, work can be done to identify all of the forces that the person will be challenging in this step, and the full significance of this as a migration of identity can be explored. A fuller appreciation of these forces and of the significance of this migration contributes to establishing a greater readiness for the journey. However, despite the close attention to this, whether or not all of these forces have been sufficiently identified, and whether or not an adequate grasp of the significance of this migration has been achieved, cannot be determined ahead of departure – there is always a strong possibility that the person will turn back.

As well as the attention that is given to preparations for the separation, it is important to engage in some predictions of the experiences that are to be had in the liminal phase – the betwixt and between that is characterised by significant periods of confusion and disorientation, and at times by despair and desperation – and in making preparations that will assist persons to see these experiences through to reincorporation.

Immediately prior to stepping into these journeys, and as they are taking their first steps, persons frequently feel their spirits rising with the new hopes for a life differently lived. However, following this, persons invariably find themselves crashing into a trough of confusion and despair. This is usually interpreted as a physiological phenomenon, one that is associated with withdrawal of the substance. However, although this physiological phenomenon is usually significant, this does not entirely account for this crash. In stepping into this journey, persons are breaking from the known, detaching from a familiar sense of the self, and they suddenly find themselves at a loss to know how to deal with the world. If persons do not understand this experience in the context of the liminal phase of the journey, it will be read as regress. Under these circumstances, with hopes not initially realised, life under the thrall of addiction and/or the excessive consumption of substances will often become a more attractive proposition than perseverance in efforts to revise one's relationship with these substances.

Although considerable attention is given to the mapping of this journey, and to preparations for the separation, liminal and reincorporation phases, it is important that persons understand that turning back remains a distinct possibility. There are ways of understanding this turning back, and preparing for this eventuality, that don't construct this as failure, that don't contribute to that 'back to square one' experience that is shaming of persons and that is so undermining of hope and of future efforts. Turning back can be understood as the outcome of an insufficient appreciation of the forces that are inciting of the consumption of substances, of gaps in the preparations made for sustaining one though the rigours of the liminal phase, and so on. It can also be understood that all attempts at migrations of this sort contribute to the development of knowledges and the skills of the sort that are necessary for the successful completion of the journey, and that these will contribute to persons being better prepared on future attempts.

Other maps

It is often helpful to provide persons with maps of the journeys made by others. Although these other maps will not accurately represent the specific ups and downs to be experienced by the person who is undertaking preparations, it none-the-less provides the person with some account of what it is that is ahead of them, and provides some guide to these preparations. These other maps also provide a measure of reassurance to persons when in the liminal phase and finding themselves in a trough of confusion and despair – this was only to be predicted, and others have been there, survived this, and have gone onto better things.

Apart from the provision of maps of similar journeys, there is the option of inviting others along for a meeting or two with the purpose of interviewing them about their experiences of migration. There is much to be learned in these interviews: what it is that has sustained others through the liminal stage, including the specific knowledges and skills that are relevant to this, the affiliations and circumstances or structures that provided necessary support, and so on. These can be interviews of persons who have undergone various migrations – geographical, national, cultural, and, of course, migrations of identity in relation to breaking from addiction and/or the excessive consumption of substances. It can be particularly helpful to interview persons who undertook a migration only to turn back and then to again retrace their steps at a later time, this time completing the journey. Often those who are interviewed in this way make themselves available as a source of support and encouragement to the persons who are about to embark on this journey.

The information gathered in these interviews can significantly inform a person's preparations for their journey. These interviews also have the effect of stimulating their ingenuity and the expression of some of the knowledges and skills, relevant to transitions in life, that can be traced through their own personal history. Further explorations of these traces can render these knowledges and skills more richly described, and thus more available to be expressed in the preparations for the migration of identity, and through the liminal phase.

Formalising the rite of passage

The formalisation of this rite of passage is helpful. A forum can be established in which the person publicly announces, before assembled witnesses, their decision to break from the addiction and/or excessive consumption of substances. Here, the person can speak to their understanding of the forces that they are up against in succeeding with this decision, and can share their appreciation of the significance of the proposed journey as a migration of identity. The hazards and the insecurity associated with this migration can be drawn out. The preparations for the journey can be outlined, along with the skills and knowledges that are available to the person in navigating this transition. The assembled witnesses then contribute to a powerful acknowledgement of all this, in part achieved by a series of retellings of what has been heard. This is an acknowledgement that is significantly authenticating of the person's decision to undertake this migration, of the purposes, hopes and commitments that this decision speaks to, and of the courage, determination, knowledges and skills that will be required in the successful conclusion of the journey. At this time, these witnesses usually volunteer those resources that might be at their disposal, and that might contribute to sustaining the person through the liminal phase.

It can also be helpful to plan, in advance, for a ritual celebration that will mark the person's arrival at the phase of reincorporation – when the person will have begun to experience some sense of familiarity with other ways of being in the world, when they will again have a sense of 'being at home' in the world, but in a different place. The shape of the proposed celebration can be worked out, and a guest list can be established. Guesses can be made about the sort of stories that the person might tell of their journey, and about the sort of declaration that the person will make about their arrival at a different place in life.

Alcoholics Anonymous: A structured rite of passage

In the above discussion I have invoked the rite of passage metaphor and provided some ideas about how this can be taken up in assisting persons to revise their relationship with substances. Upon reviewing what I have written here, I found myself reflecting on what has become a particularly well established approach to addressing addictions and/or the excessive consumption of substances that is structured as a rite of passage – Alcoholics Anonymous (AA). Although the ideas that I have discussed in this paper are not directly informed by AA, and although many of the ideas and practices of narrative work directly contradict many of the ideas and practices of AA, I nevertheless have a strong respect for AA, one that now stretches back over two and a half decades. I will here share some of these reflections, doing so in the context of an acknowledgement that I cannot claim an insider's knowledge of this system.

I believe that the originators of Alcoholics Anonymous had great vision, and a profound understanding of the significance of rites of passage. At the centre of AA is a ritual event that provides for a formalisation of the stages of separation and reincorporation, and for a marking of the turning points of persons' lives. This is accompanied by the convening of forums that provide the opportunity for persons to give testimony to the decisions that they have made to break from excessive alcohol consumption, to the desires and purposes that motivate these decisions, and to tell and retell the stories of their lives before a group of witnesses, many of whom are veterans of such journeys. In this context, the responses of the witness group are powerfully acknowledging and authenticating of these decisions, desires, purposes and stories. As these decisions and stories, and these accounts of desire and purpose, become more richly described, they become more influential – they are more significantly shaping of persons' lives.

There is also so much about AA that provides a great deal of sustenance to those who are navigating the liminal phase of this journey. There is a buddy system that provides the traveller with intimate support, and a concerned community of fellow travellers who share the maps, the knowledges, and the skills that are specific to journeys of this kind. The structure of AA builds in frequent opportunities for travellers to give voice to the trials and tribulations of these journeys, and for them to experience continuing acknowledgement of the different struggles that they find themselves engaged in.

AA's responses to persons who turn back to the bottle are generally compassionate rather than judging. This is an antidote to the demoralising sense of personal failure that is so often occasioned by such U-turns, and keeps the door open on options for persons to try again, and yet again. In response to these U-turns, the AA community just goes on reaching out. This is a reaching out by persons who have 'been there', and who have a strong appreciation of the desperation that is experienced in this struggle.

In terms of explanation for why it is that persons break from substance abuse, AA privileges notions of conscious purpose, commitment, and calling. In privileging these notions, and in not joining with the contemporary habit of psychologising motives for action, AA assists persons to resist turning their lives over to the knowledges of the professional disciplines – the understanding of what it is necessary to understand does not require a submission to the 'expert' knowledges. In evoking notions of conscious purpose, commitment and calling, AA emphasises ways of life that are guided by personal ethics, formulated and re-formulated time and time again through tellings and re-tellings in a concerned community.

Alcoholics Anonymous, in the journey that it structures, in the understandings that it emphasises, and in its actual practices, has clearly had a positive impact on the lives of so many persons.

Community responses

In that contemporary culture is a culture of consumption, and in that there is an ever increasing range of substances available to us, it should not be so surprising that addiction and/or the excessive consumption of these substances is so prevalent, and that this is destroying the lives of so many persons, traumatising of their families, and wreaking havoc in our communities. In view of the burgeoning nature of this situation, I believe that it is unrealistic to expect that individual therapeutic responses will ever be able to respond adequately. The need for organised community responses is urgent.

Alcoholics Anonymous provides a community response that has assisted many persons. But, despite its success, there are many persons for whom it doesn't fit at all well. How can this fact play a part in encouraging us to join together in the exploration and development of other community approaches to assist persons to break from addictions and/or the excessive consumption of substances? Perhaps some of these explorations could be informed by alternative applications of the rite of passage metaphor.

Note

1. This piece began its life as an interview of Michael White by David Denborough. David's thoughtful questions, and his responses to an earlier draft contributed much to the shaping of what is written here.

    I would also like to acknowledge various people who read earlier drafts of this paper and offered helpful feedback and comment. In particular I would like to thank Amanda Kamsler, David Epston and Loretta Perry.

References

Turner, V. 1969: *The Ritual Process*. New York: Cornell University Press.
van Gennep, A. 1960: *The Rites of Passage*. Chicago: University of Chicago Press.

3.

Re-engaging with history:
The absent but implicit*

Many of the practices of narrative therapy provide people with options for a re-engagement with their own histories. This is not a re-engagement with history that is predominantly a reframing of people's experiences of living – a reframing that substitutes 'the glass is half empty' orientation to the events and experiences of one's life with one that proposes that 'the glass is half full'. This is also not a re-engagement with history that constitutes a revisioning of history – that is, a rewriting of history that constructs another total account of history that displaces and cancels out the original account. At times the practice of reframing can contribute to the construction of new totalisations of the historical record that are substituted for already established totalisations – a 'bad' totalisations is traded for a 'good' totalisation. And this is invariably the outcome of the practice of the revisioning of history. In this way, the practice of reframing and the practice of revisioning history both run the risk of contributing to the development of single-storied experiences of life and of identity.

Rather than reproducing a practice that has the effect of substituting one frame for another, and rather than engaging with a practice that is revisioning of

---

* This paper was presented at the Narrative Therapy and Community Work Conference, Adelaide, February, 1999.

the familiar historical records of people's lives, the practices of narrative therapy that contribute to options for a re-engagement with history bring forth multi-storied experiences of life and of identity. These practices not only contribute to an expansion of people's narrative resources, but also make it possible for them to alter their relationship with their own histories. This is not to reframe or to change history by revisioning it, but to re-engage with personal history on new terms.

There are many options that can be taken up by therapists in joining with people in significant re-engagements with their histories. One of the routes to these re-engagements with history is through the identification and rich description of that which is absent but implicit in all expressions of life; that is, through the identification and the rich description of whatever it is that makes it possible for people to give meaning to, and to put into circulation, aspects of their lived experience. The notion of the 'absent but implicit' is informed by the understanding that all expression, and the meaning that expression conveys, is not derived directly from the experience of the 'thing' that expression refers to – the accounts of life that shape expression do not represent a one-to-one correspondence with the properties that exist in whatever it is that is being described in these accounts. People's expressions of life do not apprehend the world out there as it is, whatever that world might be.

Rather, expressions of living are understood to be a phenomenon made possible by 'making things out', or by distinguishing things and giving them meaning, in relation to, or in contrast to, the meanings or descriptions of other things. By this account, there is a duality to all descriptions. Descriptions are relational, not representational – they do not directly represent the things of the world, whatever those things might be. According to this relational understanding of all description, a singular description can be considered to be the visible side of a double description. It is that which is on the other side of singular descriptions of experiences of living – that which is on the other side of what is being discerned, and upon what this discernment depends – that I am here referring to as the 'absent but implicit'. I find support for this understanding of the nature of description in the ideas of Gregory Bateson (1980) and Jaques Derrida (1978), who sought to challenge the myth of 'presence' – that is, the ideal of an unmediated knowledge of the world, of an original presence that is manifested in our expressions of life, and that is represented in the descriptions of our speech and our writing.

For example, Derrida developed a deconstructive method of reading texts that brought forth the absent signs or descriptions that are relied upon for a text to establish its meanings. An assumption of this textual analysis is that every term of description contains both itself and its opposite or its other, and that the relationship between these terms can be identified through a close reading of the text. In making reference to Derrida in this way I am not proposing that life is just a text, but suggesting that by a close listening to people's expressions we might have the opportunity to engage with them in conversations that are identifying of the relationship between what they discern in these expressions, and the absent but implicit descriptions without which these discernments could not be arrived at.

It can be helpful to assume that many of the discernments that people make about the state of their own lives and that they share with therapists are discernments that implicate or that are dependent upon the unstated – upon that which is absent but implicit. With this assumption, therapists can engage in an inquiry that contributes to the identification of the absent but implicit, and to its rich description. Let me offer an example: Let's say a person consults me about 'despair'. I will first want to understand as best I can their experience of this despair, and how it manifests itself in their lives. I will also want to understand as best I can the contexts of this despair, which can include socioeconomic conditions and the power relations of local culture. These contexts can be subsequently foregrounded and addressed in a variety of ways.

But I will also be interested in what it is that this despair speaks to, or what it is a testimony to, in terms of the absent but implicit – in how the person came to identify and to represent their experience in this way, in the circumstances or conditions that made it possible for them to discern despair. This interest in what despair speaks to in terms of the absent but implicit does not constitute a departure from the conversation at hand – this does not introduce conversations that are discontinuous with those conversations that open space for people's expressions of despair. Rather, this interest is taken up in these conversations in response to the particularities of the person's expressions of despair – in these expressions are to be found the traces of a multiplicity of unstated signs or descriptions that have contributed to the possibility of the discernment of despair.

How is this interest in the absent but implicit taken up in response to a person's expressions of despair? In speaking of their despair, a person might say: 'I don't think that I can carry on any more', or 'I have reached a point at which I have given up', or 'I can no longer see a future for myself'. That which is absent but implicit in the discernment of despair might be identified through the introduction of questions like: 'You said that you could no longer continue on. Would it be okay with you if I asked some questions about your sense of what you had been continuing on with up to this point? Or perhaps about what it was that you had been depending on to see you through up to now?'; 'You said that you have given up. Could I ask some questions about what it is you are giving up on? Or perhaps about what it is that you are getting separated from, or losing touch with, that had been important to you?'; or 'You said that you can't see a future for yourself any more? Would it be okay for me to ask you about what possibilities you had seen for your future? And how, at least to a point, this has been sustaining of your life up to this time? Or perhaps about what it was that had made it possible for you, until recently, to keep this future in sight?'

That which is absent but implicit that these inquiries bring forth can include 'hopes' that things would be different in one's life, 'promises' of better things to come, 'dreams' of a life lived more fully, 'anticipations' of arriving at a particular destination in life, 'visions' of new possibilities, 'wishes' to be elsewhere, to be in other territories of life, and so on. Once identified, these accounts can be richly described. This rich description is achieved in conversations that trace the trajectory of that which had been absent but implicit in people's expressions of despair, in explorations of the history of people's relationship with the previously absent but implicit. These conversations can be shaped by questions like: 'How did you manage to hold onto this hope for as long as you did, despite everything that you went through that was discouraging of it?', 'What possibilities did this hope bring to your life that you would not have otherwise conceived of?'.

Questions can also be introduced that encourage people to identity the skills and the knowledges that they engaged with in maintaining their relationship with hope, or with whatever else it was that was unstated: 'From what you have told me, I understand that there have been times when you were nearly dispossessed of this hope?', 'Can you recall the steps that you took to reclaim it?', 'Do you have any idea about the know-how that might have sustained you in taking these steps?'.

Rather than developing a naturalistic account of whatever it is that was absent but implicit in people's expressions, narrative conversations contribute to the rich description of this through an inquiry that is identifying of the significant historical conditions – of those historical conditions that provided a context for the discernments of people's expressions. For example, in the case of a previously unstated account of hope that contributed to the discernment of despair, an inquiry of this sort can be introduced through questions like: 'It is my understanding that you were not simply resigned to your lot in life. Could I ask you some questions about how you were introduced to the hope that things would one day be different for you?', 'Or perhaps some questions about what put you in touch with the fact that the lot that you had been served up with in life was not all that there was to life?'

The historical conditions that provide the contexts for such a discernment are many and varied. A person may have had some direct personal experience of life lived differently, or may have experienced some acknowledgement from a significant figure that they deserved a better life (from a peer, a sibling, a parent or some other relative, or perhaps a teacher or a shopkeeper). Or the experiences that provided the person with a basis for this discernment may have been more vicariously had – for example, through an intimate engagement with a novel, or perhaps in witnessing the circumstances of life in a friend's family. Once identified, these historical conditions can be reproduced. For example, significant figures from a person's history who provided a basis for this discernment can be re-engaged with – this can be a material re-engagement, in the case of inviting these figures to join the therapeutic conversations in one way or another, or it can be non-material, in the case of evoking the presences and voices of these figures. Or, the therapist can join with people in the shared reading of and reflection on those novels that have provided the basis for this discernment. And so on.

A challenge to naturalistic accounts of identity

In these conversations, whatever it is that was unstated in people's expressions is not routinely taken into naturalistic accounts of life and of identity in the way that it would be in conversations that are shaped by the humanist discourses – for example, that which was absent but implicit is not construed as the manifestation of an irrepressible and resilient human nature, or as an expression of an essential self that is considered to exist at the centre of personhood. To put this another way, it is not only the discernments that people give expression to at the outset of therapeutic conversations that are not given the status of a presence, but, as well, that which is absent by implicit in these discernments is not assigned such a status. It is my understanding that these humanist renderings of life and identity have the potential to dead end therapeutic inquiry as they can be obscuring of significant knowledges and skills of living that have been generated in the histories of people's lives, and of the important historical conditions that have provided a context for these people to arrive at a whole range of discernments. On account of this, evoking presences like specific personal properties or attributes to explain the previously absent but implicit often constructs relatively thin conclusions about people's lives, and shuts the door on options for extra-ordinary inquiry in therapeutic conversations.

To engage, in this way, in conversations that do not contribute to the development of a naturalistic account of what is absent but implicit in people's descriptions of their experience, that do not contribute to interpreting the absent but implicit as the manifestation of a presence like a personal property or attribute, is not to take a position that is dishonouring of people's preferred identity conclusions – 'I guess that this hope is an expression of my resilience'. In the context of these therapeutic conversations, these identity conclusions are celebrated. But they are also unpacked in ways that render them substantially more significant. These identity conclusions are understood to be the emblems of particular modes of life and thought that are associated with a range of knowledges and skills of living that have been generated in the histories of people's lives, with certain purposes that also have a historical trajectory, and with specific themes and commitments around which people's lives are linked to the lives of others. Conversations that unpack these conclusions about presence contribute to the rich description of life and of identity, and to new options for action in the world that would not otherwise be available to people.

Double listening and multi-storied conversations

The engagement with this interest in the absent but implicit requires, and is reinforcing of, a double listening on behalf of the therapist. It is in the context of this double listening that people experience being doubly or multiply heard. This is a context in which people find that there is space for them to express their experience of whatever it is that troubles them. And, as well, it is in this context that they have the opportunity to explore the unstated; that is, whatever it is that this discernment speaks to. In this way, the engagement with this interest in the absent but implicit contributes to therapeutic conversations as double- or multi-storied conversations.

It is in the space provided in the context of double- or multi-storied conversations that people often find new opportunity to speak of the effects of whatever it is that they have found troublesome – whether this be disqualification, trauma, subjugation, marginalisation and so on – and to express the distress that is associated with these experiences. It is also in the space that is provided by double- or multi-storied conversations that people have an opportunity to step into alternative identity conclusions that challenge those negative accounts of identity that have been constructed in the context of disqualification, trauma, subjugation and marginalisation, and to explore some of the knowledges and skills of living that are associated with these alternative identity conclusions. This is an important consideration, for it is in single-storied conversations that are informed by modern notions of catharsis that there is always the risk of contributing to re-traumatisation and to renewed distress, and to the reinforcement of those negative identity conclusions that are so often the outcome of being in a subject position in relation to experiences that are traumatic or disqualifying. I do not believe that it is acceptable for therapeutic conversations to contribute to re-traumatisation or renewed distress, or to the reinforcement of people's negative identity conclusions.

Categories of re-engagement

The exploration of the sort of options that I have outlined here for re-engagements with history can contribute to the construction of 'categories of re-engagement'. The construction of these categories can be helpful in that this provides a guide to practice. But more than this – in constructing these categories we are drawing out certain distinctions that provide a foundation for establishing yet further distinctions that would not have otherwise been generated. In multiplying these 'categories of re-engagement' we can increase the range of available options for therapeutic conversations. In the following discussion I will provide some examples of just a few categories of re-engagement.

Beyond burden

Julie sought consultation over a pervasive feeling of incompleteness and a general dissatisfaction with her life. As part of this she experienced a vague but compelling sense that things were 'just not fair', and that they never would be. She had struggled with this sense for as long as she could remember, and was finding this increasingly preoccupying and frustrating. She didn't think that she had any excuse for feeling this way – by any measure, according to Julie, the present circumstances of her life were good.

After encouraging Julie to more fully describe these feelings of incompleteness and dissatisfaction, and after gathering some account of the effects of these feelings on her life, I asked her to share with me any understandings that she had of this experience. Julie said that she really only had one understanding of this, and that she thought this had been attended to already – some difficulties that Julie had experienced as a young woman had been diagnosed as a neurosis that was considered to be the outcome of having been a 'parentified child'. She had, according to this account, carried a burden in her childhood and adolescence that had not only constituted a substantial deprivation, but had arrested her development in significant ways. Julie said that she had, in the context of psychotherapy, worked through what had been determined to be her issues on several occasions – including her unconscious lament for and her grief over her lost childhood, and her anger over the injustice of the deprivation and over the burdening of her life – and although she knew there still might be more to be resolved, she 'had to confess' that she was 'sick of it all'.

I asked Julie if she would fill me in on some details that could help me become familiar with what these understandings related to, and before long she was describing her life as a child. From the outset of their union, things didn't go very well for her parents. They'd had their hopes and dreams, but their marriage was rejected by both of their families, and Julie didn't think that her parents had been at all prepared for the isolation that they fell into as an outcome of this. From rural Victoria, (one of the Australian states) they moved to Melbourne, hoping for a lucky break. But none came. They were now poor. And from this shaky beginning, things just got worse. Soon after the birth of Julie's younger sister, her father became ill, and could no longer do the seasonal work that the family had relied upon for income. Eventually he was diagnosed with a congenital condition and was, to use Julie's description, 'invalided out'.

Then things got worse still. Julie's mother began to have difficulties coping with everyday tasks and gradually became depressed. Before long she could hardly function at all. In response to things falling apart in this way, Julie took on more parenting responsibilities in relation to her younger sister, Jane. She also became responsible for many of the general household tasks that had always been managed by her mother. Over the next year or two Julie's school attendance became irregular, and the family lived constantly under the threat of welfare action – this was the threat of taking Julie and her sister into what was referred to as 'care'. As Julie was recounting this episode of her life, she recalled that on one occasion the school authorities didn't notice, for a period of five months, that she hadn't been attending school. Over this time there were no incursions into the family by 'the welfare', and it turned out to be one of the happiest times of her childhood that Julie could remember. In recalling this, Julie said that to this very day she didn't know from where her mother had managed to summon up the where-with-all to avoid this welfare action.

Julie's father died in a nursing home in her fifteenth year. His death barely caused a ripple. In the last years of his life he wasn't even a shadow of his former self – this was so to the point that he was barely recognisable even to family members. Julie 'soldiered on through all of this', getting the odd job here and there to supplement the family's pension. Somehow she managed to get through most of her schooling and supported her sister in doing likewise.

Gradually her mother got her life together a little – after a fashion at least. She wasn't well, but was starting to do some things for herself. Now a young woman, Julie 'struck out on her own', and for a time her relationship with her mother was quite strained for this. Although things were getting better between the two of them by the time Julie was in her mid-twenties, some of the strain in their relationship remained until her mother's death, at which time Julie was thirty-seven years of age.

Julie was now talking about the predicament that she was finding herself in on account of all of this. And she had lots of questions: How was she going to ever deal with this burden that she carried? Would she ever be able to get back what she had lost? What she had been deprived of? All of that which had been taken from her? Was she condemned to this sense of incompleteness, and to the restlessness that was associated with this, that was an outcome of this burden? Would she always feel that things were so unfair? Could this possibly be resolved? She was despairing that her future would take the form of one long paralysing lament.

In this expression of her predicament, Julie had discerned deprivation, loss, dispossession, incompleteness, burden and unfairness. Any of these discernments could be taken into explorations that would be potentially identifying of that which is absent but implicit. My curiosity was most drawn to Julie's expressions of unfairness, perhaps because at the outset of our conversation she had strongly emphasised her sense that things were 'just not fair'. I asked Julie to talk more about this unfairness, and, in response, she said that she had a sense that, no matter what she did, she would never feel recognised and valued. I reflected on what I had heard, and asked Julie if I was correct in concluding that she had a wish for some acknowledgement. Julie instantaneously confirmed this, stating that it was a 'longing' for acknowledgement. That which was absent but implicit in Julie's discernment about things being 'just not fair' was now identified as a longing for acknowledgement.

Rather than engaging with a naturalistic account of this longing that would interpret it as a manifestation of human nature, I asked some questions that encouraged Julie to richly describe it, and to trace its history in her life. I was curious about the fact that she had never abandoned this quest for acknowledgement, despite the fact that it contributed to very considerable dissatisfaction and frustration. How had she preserved her relationship with this longing for acknowledgement? I also wished to understand how it was that, in the circumstances of her history, she was able to identify acknowledgement as a valued experience. I asked Julie if she could recount any experiences of her life that might have provided her with some familiarity with acknowledgement, that might have been confirming of this as a desirable experience. Before long Julie was sharing with me some slim stories about her sister and her mother's acknowledgement of what she had contributed to their lives.

After exploring these stories, I asked Julie if it would be okay to ask some questions about her parenting skills, about her skills in nurturing others, that were evident in these stories – about her skills in caring, in loving, in acknowledgement, in attending, in soothing, in going the extra mile, in building environments of understanding in the face of invalidation, in contributing to contexts of acceptance that provide an antidote to experiences of marginalisation and rejection, and so on. 'After all', I said, 'You have a long history of parenting, and it seems like this got your sister and your mother through what they might not have otherwise got through'.

Julie seemed taken aback by my comments. 'Are you for real!', she exclaimed. To this I replied: 'Now, that is something that I have never been very sure about. Others haven't been sure about that either. I know this because I've been asked that question before, but not quite as graciously as you have asked it. Now perhaps this graciousness is just another one of those parenting skills that I was referring to, and I am grateful for this right now.' Julie grinned widely. Before long I was collecting wonderful stories that reflected a rich tradition of knowledges and skills of parenting that Julie had very significantly contributed to the development of. Not only were these knowledges and skills richly-described in this conversation, but some of the questions I had the opportunity to ask precipitated a powerful acknowledgement of the essential contribution that these knowledges and skills made to Julie's mother, her sister and her father in getting through what they got through, and to what was beyond this – for example, the steps that Julie's mother was able to take in at last getting her own life back on the track that she wanted it to be on.

Julie seemed electrified in this conversation. I had the sense that, in this re-engagement with history, she had already entered a different territory of her life. Where was she? What was she experiencing? Julie said that she was feeling joy of the sort that one could only hope for in attending a celebration of something really important. 'Now, that's an interesting idea', I said, 'Because it fits with a thought that I was having about the possibility of getting together with some folks who also have insider knowledge of the sort of experiences of life that you have had. These folks also happen to be older parentified children, just as you are. And these folks also just happen to like celebrations.' I shared my thoughts about the shape of a proposed get-together with some other people who had been considered 'parentified children', and Julie was enthusiastic to give it a go.

I called Ted, Joanne and Shirley (33 years, 42 years, and 67 years respectively), who'd all had considerable parenting experience when they were children, and who had consulted me in times past. These were among a number of people who had been willing to have their names entered into my register of parentified children so that they might play a part in my work with others who were to consult me over the issues associated with this status. I filled them in on the details that Julie had granted me permission to pass on, and talked about the proposed meeting. Joanne, Ted and Shirley unhesitatingly accepted the invitation to be part of such an event, and after some negotiations we arrived at a mutually suitable time to meet. This meeting duly took place and was structured around the definitional ceremony metaphor (see White, 1999). In Joanne, Ted and Shirley's presence, I interviewed Julie about her parenting career, about the specifics of her parenting knowledges and skills, and about what possibilities these had brought to her world. I then asked Julie to sit back, and invited Ted and Joanne and Shirley to retell what they had heard. This retelling, was, in part, structured by my questions: 'As you listened to Julie's story, what most captured your imagination?', 'What did you hear that engaged your attention?', 'What struck a chord for you?', 'What images have Julie's words evoked for you?', 'How was it that you could relate to what you were relating to as you listened to Julie?', 'What did you come to understand about the knowledges and skills that were developed by Julie?', 'In what ways do you feel touched by Julie's expressions, and in what ways are these rippling into your own lives?', 'What was it about your own histories that was resonating with these expressions?', 'How are Julie's expressions effecting you?', and so on. In Shirley, Ted and Joanne's retelling, the stories of Julie's life were linked to the stories of their lives around shared themes, purposes and commitments.

I also asked this trio other questions: 'What difference do you think it would have made if the welfare had powerfully acknowledged Julie's skills and

Re-engaging with history: The absent but implicit 47

knowledges of parenting and had found ways of supporting her in these?', 'What difference do you think it would have made if the authorities had not only acknowledged and supported Julie in her parenting of her sister, her mother, and her father, but had also arranged for her to have time out on occasions?', 'For circumstances to be arranged that would have allowed her to go off duty every now and then?'.

Julie was then invited to talk about what she had heard in these retellings of Joanne, Ted and Shirley. During this time, I had the opportunity to ask some questions: 'Would you talk about what you heard in the responses of Shirley, Ted and Joanne?', 'Of all this, what most caught your attention?', 'What is your understanding about why it was that you most strongly related to these aspects of the retellings?', 'Were there particular realisations that came to you, that were connected to these aspects?', 'Did these retellings evoke any images of your life, of your identity, or of your place in the world?', 'If so, would you be prepared to describe these images?', 'What do these images touch on in terms of the history of your life?', 'Do they light up certain memories?', 'Is there anything about your life that you more highly value, that you might be more acknowledging of, as an outcome of these retellings?', 'What was it like for you to hear something from Shirley, Ted and Joanne about how your expressions had touched their lives?', and so on.

As an outcome of these tellings and retellings something highly significant happened for Julie. Something had 'clicked'. Something had 'come together for the first time'. That pervasive sense of being incomplete had 'gone up in smoke'. Julie no longer felt the burden that had been so pressing for so long. She experienced relief and joy in a newfound sense that her life 'would not be lived out as one long paralysing lament'. A void had 'gone'. Over three more meetings Julie had the opportunity to more fully embrace the knowledges of life and the skills of living that she had developed as a child in the context of her family, and, as well, some of the possibilities that this had brought to her life, and could bring to her future. She experienced the realness of these knowledges and skills, and no longer conceived of and dismissed her parentified child status as just a role that she had played. For Julie there were now pros and cons to her parentified child status, and, in the balance, she had decided that she wouldn't want to forsake what it was that this status had brought to her life.

When Julie felt ready, she invited her sister to join us to catch her up on these conversations, and to contribute to further retellings – but that is another story.

Beyond rejection

Lyndon consulted me about what he termed his 'inadequacy'. He said that this personal inadequacy had 'dogged' him for a considerable part of his life, despite numerous efforts to deal with it. He had thought long and hard about it, and had even ventured to talk with others about it from time to time. It was his understanding that this sense of personal inadequacy was the outcome of his father's rejection of him as a child and young man. This rejection was principally expressed in what Lyndon read as disinterest. Lyndon's father was rarely present in his life, and, try as he might – and he certainly tried hard (in fact, from the stories that Lyndon told me about this, I gained a sense that his persistence had been quite remarkable) – Lyndon was never able to please his father. In the early part of our conversation we explored what Lyndon understood to be the effects of this rejection on his life. It was during this time that I asked Lyndon to reflect back on what he had said about his inadequacy – what sort of light did our conversation throw on this? In response to this question he reinterpreted this inadequacy as an experience of absence – this was the outcome of a prevailing sense of something being absent from his life.

Lyndon had discerned inadequacy, rejection, disinterest and absence. Any of these discernments could be taken into explorations that would be potentially identifying of that which is absent but implicit in them. I was curious. How was it that Lyndon had so clearly discerned rejection, and why hadn't he been resigned to his father's apparent rejection of him? Why hadn't he come to take for granted his father's non-presence in his life? Why had he continued to experience this absence so keenly? Such questions are informed by a refusal of naturalistic accounts of this sort of phenomenon. In this circumstance, this refusal made it possible for me to turn away from the reading of this sense of rejection and of something being absent from his life as an experience that could only be expected, as an expression of the fact that Lyndon's needs hadn't been met, or of the fact that it would only be human for him to be feeling this way. Too much is obscured by explanations that defer to the rules of human nature. In refusing such naturalistic accounts, I was able to engage Lyndon in explorations of that which was absent but implicit – the unstated that made it possible for him to draw distinctions in his experience, and that had made it possible for him to conclude that something was missing from his life.

I began to ask Lyndon questions about what might have sensitised him to his father's rejection of him, and to his father's absence from his life. For a while our conversation meandered through Lyndon's history. He had grown up in a small country town. His parents were relatively poor, and both worked hard in manual jobs. He spent a lot of time alone – some of this time fishing in the local dam that was some distance from his family home. In this account of Lyndon's history, there were a number of potential points of entry to conversations that might address some of the questions that I had been asking. Of all of these possibilities, I chose fishing. Fishing isn't something that children just come to. Fishing is not an expression of human nature. It is something that children, and more often boys, are introduced to in one way or another – through stories, by parents and other caretakers, by other children, and so on. 'How were you introduced to fishing?', I wanted to know. After reflecting on this for a while, Lyndon told me a story about the town's post-master – an old but energetic man who had a love for fishing, and who had, through happenstance, introduced Lyndon to this love. Lyndon remembered that the post-master was a gruff and matter-of-fact sort of man who didn't say a lot. He didn't even like big fishing stories. In the first place, Lyndon had been a little afraid of him. He always gave Lyndon the impression that in allowing Lyndon to accompany him he was actually being granted a very significant privilege – that in this act, something of great value was being bestowed on Lyndon that he should take care to properly respect.

As we reflected on this some, Lyndon said, 'You know, it's kind of strange, but as we talk about this I find myself thinking that this was acknowledging of me. I think I must have realised even at the time, at some level at least, that the postmaster wouldn't have let just anybody join him. But now I have a fuller realisation of this'. I asked Lyndon how this present fuller realisation of a historical but slim realisation was effecting him in our conversation – what was his immediate experience of this? In response to this question Lyndon choked up with emotion, and for a while he couldn't speak. We sat there in silence for a period of time – it must have been more than ten minutes, but I doubt that either of us could have gauged this at the time. I had the sense that we were together in some sort of liminal space.

When Lyndon did begin to speak, he told me that he had felt something shift for him. He said that it was difficult for him to find the words to speak of this, but knew that the sense of absence that we had talked about at the beginning of the interview wasn't as intense as it had been. 'Could I ask some more questions about your connection with the post-master?' (who, by the way, had retired and moved to Sydney when Lyndon was still a young boy). Lyndon said that this would be okay, so I began to ask what I now refer to as re-membering questions (White, 1997). At an earlier time I termed these experience of experience questions (White, 1988).

- *What is your sense of what this inclusion brought to your life?*
- *What is your understanding of what it was that the post-master was acknowledging or recognising about you?*
- *What did this put you in touch with that you might have learned to appreciate about yourself?*
- *Do you know why it was that the postmaster included you in his life in this way?*
- *What do you think it was that he saw in you that might not have been so visible to your father?*
- *How do you think this inclusion could be explained. What do you think your presence might have brought to the postmasters life?*
- *What's your guess about what you contributed to this man's life that your father missed out on?*
- *In what way might your father's life have been different had he been available to what the postmaster was available to?*

These were questions that addressed the postmaster's contribution to Lyndon's life by way of his recognition of Lyndon, and Lyndon's contribution to the life of the postmaster. These questions also addressed and contributed to the acknowledgement of what was an ever-present potential for Lyndon to contribute to his father's life, if only this man had taken the steps to open the door to him. In the conversation that was shaped by these questions, that which was absent but implicit in Lyndon's discernment of rejection and absence was richly described; that is, experiences of life that are read as examples of inclusion and acceptance.

At the risk of labouring the point, here I will again emphasise the significance, for therapeutic conversations, of the refusal of naturalistic accounts of the events of life. I do this because these accounts have come to be so taken-for-granted in contemporary understandings of people's actions and identities that it can be difficult to think outside of them. While I believe that these naturalistic accounts have the potential to dead-end our work with the people who consult us, the refusal of these accounts opens the door to virtually endless possibilities for what I have at times referred to as 're-authoring conversations'. For example, to routinely engage in naturalistic accounts of developments in life invariably renders invisible the contribution of the 'other' to the conditions of possibility for developments in a person's life, to a person's stock of knowledges of life and skills of living, and quells curiosity about how things came to be the way they are.

In not stepping into a naturalistic account of these historical developments on Lyndon's life, rather than making an assumption that Lyndon's connection with the postmaster was simply a testimony to his needs and to the good grace of the postmaster, I wondered what else this might have been a testimony to in terms of the contribution of the 'other'. In this circumstance I was thinking about Lyndon's father as this other, and I became curious about whatever else might be absent but implicit in this development of the connection between Lyndon and the postmaster.

This curiosity about this absent but implicit contributed to new questions: 'Why hadn't your father obstructed this association with the postmaster?', 'Why hadn't he denied this to you?', 'Fathers who have little to do with their sons do at times act out of a position of righteous indignation when it comes to their sons' connections to other men. They can act from a sense of defensiveness and from a sentiment of control, in ways that are characterised as jealousy', 'How come your father did not insist on mediating your relationship with the outside world in this way?'. These questions aroused

Lyndon's interest, but, as they invited him to think outside of what he routinely thought in relation to matters of his personal history, he did not have any ready-made answers. Our time together was coming to an end, so I wrote down these questions and Lyndon took them away with him to ponder over.

I met with Lyndon again two weeks later. Something significant had taken place in his life – I knew this instantly from his composure in the waiting room. I learned that soon after our first meeting, Lyndon sought out his uncle James – his father's youngest brother – who was aged and infirm and living in a nursing home. Lyndon took a chance and shared with his uncle the story of the conversation we'd had. He then raised with his uncle the question: 'My father could have felt put out by my connection with the postmaster. Do you have any idea of why my father didn't disrupt this?' Nothing could have prepared Lyndon for Uncle James's response.

In addressing this question, Uncle James informed Lyndon that his father had, on several occasions, when in the local hotel while drinking together, confided his sense of inadequacy about fatherhood. He just didn't know what to do in his relationship with Lyndon. He had told Uncle James that he knew he had 'hurt the boy', but had no idea how to make things better. He felt at sea in the presence of his son – 'all thumbs and no artistry'. He thought it was the war's fault (Second World War). That it had wrecked him in ways that he could hardly fathom. He had reached the conclusion that it was better for him to stay out of his sons life as best he could. It would be better for Lyndon this way. Although he had never said so, Uncle James thought that Lyndon's father had felt secretly relieved by the postmaster's connection with Lyndon.

Some gifts are tragic gifts, but they are gifts none the less. Staying out of his son's life, and not interfering in Lyndon's connection with the postmaster, could be recognised by Lyndon as the one gift that his father believed he had to give to his son. Following our second meeting, Lyndon went back to the town of his childhood, and visited his father's grave site for the first time in many years. And on the very next ANZAC day (the occasion upon which the veterans of World War's One and Two, and the Vietnam War, march in the streets of the capital cities around Australia and New Zealand) he marched in the parade. He found joining the ANZAC march to be an overwhelmingly emotional experience, and later identified this as marking a significant turning point in his life. As a result of this, he very substantially broke free of that sense of inadequacy that had 'dogged his life' for so long.

Later in our conversations there were options for Lyndon to re-engage with personal history in ways that made it possible for him to also revise the terms of his relationship with his mother. This too had significantly positive effects in his life. But that is another story.

Beyond survival

Jane came to see me at the insistence of her cousin, Sue. Sue was a mental health nurse who experienced a shock recognition of Jane when she was admitted to hospital following a suicide attempt that very nearly claimed her life. Sue and Jane hadn't seen each other for three decades. As young children they'd had infrequent but enjoyable contact – between them there seemed to be a mutual but unspoken understanding of many things.

Over many years, Sue had heard snippets of information about the predicaments of Jane's life – about the extended episodes of depression, about the cutting, about the attempts on her own life, and about the frequent admissions to hospital. But Sue had been frightened of the spectre drawn by these snippets, and was herself hard pressed in her efforts to get her own life together under circumstances that were far from easy. Nonetheless, Jane had 'been on her conscience', and when she had recognised her on the ward, newly admitted and in a very sorry state, Sue had immediately decided that she would make it her business to lend Jane whatever assistance she could muster.

In response to Sue's recognition of her, Jane had initially fled into withdrawal, overwhelmed by shame. But Sue had persisted in her efforts to make contact, and after several days Jane had reciprocated Sue's recognition of her, and subsequently began to participate in Sue's reminiscing about the times they'd been together in their childhood – Sue even had Jane laughing on an occasion or two. Before long, Sue was insisting that Jane come to meet with me. Jane was quite reluctant about the idea and did her best to discourage Sue's enthusiasm for it. But Sue wouldn't be discouraged. In the end Jane agreed 'to go along for the ride'.

Here they were. Jane curled up in a foetal position on the chair, silently rocking. Sue filling me in on things as best she could, catching me up on her hopes for our conversation and on her feelings of apprehension on Jane's behalf. Jane had requested that Sue speak for her, and wanted me to know that she was sceptical about this new initiative – she had predicted that nothing good would come of it, that we would simply be a raking over of lots of bad things that had been raked over many times before, and that by the end of it she would only feel worse. Sue was also personally concerned about the possibility that Jane might feel worse at the end of our meeting, and knew from her history that it was at times like this that Jane was most likely to cut herself.

In response to these predictions and concerns, I said that this raking over of things may not be at all necessary, and that I would like for us to work out a way that I could be kept in touch with how things were going for Jane at all times during the course of our conversation. This way, should Jane begin to feel worse at any point, I would have the opportunity to take responsibility for the shape of the conversation, and to introduce some explorations that would get us onto a track that might have a more desirable outcome for her.

Sue then began to share some details of Jane's experiences of life, those that Jane had wanted me informed of: the abuse that she had been subject to by her father and grandfather; the isolation she had experienced through all of this; the disqualification and pain that she had been subject to in the two or three efforts she had made to form a relationship in the adult years of her life; her diagnoses and the history of her 'psychiatric illness', and so on. Soon Jane began to join Sue in her rendition of this account, and as she did so, her rocking became more vigorous.

In this conversation I became aware of the fact that Jane had two understandings of what she had been through. There was a dominant understanding that 'she deserved the abuse' – indeed, that she was culpable for the abuse that she had been subject to. But there was a secondary and relatively slim understanding that was also present in her expressions of the trauma that had provided the context of her life as a child and as a young woman – an understanding that what was being done to her was wrong. It was this secondary understanding that particularly caught my attention, and I asked about its history, and about what it was that this understanding spoke to. After some discussion, Jane and Sue concluded that this understanding was shaped by a degree of awareness of the nature of injustice, but that this awareness was insignificant in relation to Jane's sense of personal culpability and shame.

I was curious about that which was absent but implicit in this discernment of injustice, and in response to this I began to ask some questions: 'Although you mostly blamed yourself for what you were being put through, and believed that you deserved this, I understand that you never totally lost sight of the fact that it was also an injustice. Would it be okay for me to ask you some questions about how you came to realise that this was an injustice?', 'And about how you managed to hold onto this understanding despite everything that was denying of it?'. To pursue this line was acceptable to Jane, and before long we were in a conversation about what this said about what she had stood for over all the years of her life, and about what she had done that reflected her position on 'justice'. This stand for justice was identified as what had been absent but implicit in Jane's discernment of injustice.

The conversation turned towards a fuller tracing of the trajectory of this stand for justice through the history of Jane's life. In response to some further questions, Jane and Sue began to identify many more manifestations of this stand for justice, and linked this not just to Jane's survival, but also to her ability to perceive the injustices being done to others, her sense of outrage at this, and her wish to do something that would make a difference in the world. In this conversation there were opportunities to engage in a re-reading of what had been interpreted by others as passive/aggressive and hostile/dependent behaviour on Jane's behalf. I openly wondered how these acts might be understood in the light of her position on matters of justice. In response to this inquiry, Sue initially, soon to be joined by Jane, began to represent these as acts of subversion inspired by Jane's position on justice; acts of subversion in a range of contexts where there was a substantial inequality in power and in which a direct and open challenge to any action that was unjust or unfair would, in all likelihood, be responded to with acts of retribution. Over the course of our meeting, Jane's stand for justice was more richly described – it was, for the first time, acknowledged by her as a 'commitment' and a 'passion', and, by Sue, as 'perhaps even a calling' in Jane's life. As our meeting came to a close I asked Jane about how she was feeling. She said that she was surprised not to be feeling badly. And yes, she would be interested in meeting again.

At the outset of the following meeting we had a conversation about the historical circumstances that had contributed to Jane's appreciation of justice, which had provided the conditions of possibility for her discernment of injustice. In reflecting on this, Jane suddenly had a realisation, one that implicated Sue – there had been an unstated knowing between them about matters of fairness and unfairness. As well, there had been some acknowledgement about, and disapproval of, what each other had been subject to by others. This also hadn't been directly spoken of in the history of their connection with each other, but had been expressed in much of their play together. Sue confirmed this by talking about some of the particularities of this play, and about the themes featured in this. This appeared to be a sparkling discovery for both Jane and Sue. In further explorations of the history of their shared commitment to justice, Sue also implicated a novel that she and Jane had shared when they were children. The central character in this novel was a heroine who had a strong consciousness of what was fair and what wasn't, and whose actions were a powerful expression of this consciousness. They decided to obtain a copy of this novel and to read it together.

I had presented Jane and Sue with the option of organising the third meeting around a definitional ceremony structure, one that would incorporate the participation of an outsider-witness group (White, 1999). I described this option, and responded to Jane and Sue's questions about it. Although they initially felt a degree of apprehension about the proposal, they both thought that it would be worth giving a try. Before proceeding, I suggested that it might be a good idea for them to speak with some people who had experienced being at the centre of such a ceremony. I arranged for this, and in response Sue called to confirm their decision to proceed with the idea. The outsider-witness group that was present for this third meeting was made up of workers from the health/welfare/counselling fields who were attending a week-long intensive course on narrative therapy at Dulwich Centre. In the first part of this meeting Jane and Sue engaged in a telling of what they deemed to be the most significant aspects of the story of Jane's life, with considerable emphasis on the alternative version of Jane's identity that had featured strongly in our therapeutic conversations, and in the telling of an account of the history of their camaraderie, of the experiences that had contributed to their discernment of injustice, and of the recent developments in their lives and in their connection with each other. In response to this, the outsider-witness group's retelling was powerfully authenticating of the many identity claims that were expressed by Jane and Sue. In addition to this, upon hearing a couple of the members of the outsider-witness group speak of some of the new considerations and learnings that they might take from this meeting into their work with others who had gone through experiences that were similar to Jane's, and of some of the possibilities that this might open up for these people, Jane exclaimed: 'For the first time in my life I feel that all that I have gone through hasn't been for nothing!' One of these group members followed this up, and jointly constructed, with a person who had subsequently consulted them, a letter to Jane providing specific details of the ways that her expressions had positively influenced the course of their therapeutic conversations, and, as well, had presented new options for this person to break from self-abuse.

Over several more meetings, two of which were also organised around the definitional ceremony structure, Jane steered her life onto a course that was much more in line with what she valued and with what she had determined to be her preferred purposes in life. Self-abuse was not a feature of this course.

Conclusion

I have taken this space to discuss some of the implications of the notion that expressions of life are associated with discernments that depend upon the absent but implicit – that is, unstated signs or descriptions that provide the conditions of possibility for these discernments. And yet, at the end of this article I am left with the sense that, in terms of these implications, what I have described is just a fraction of the possibilities that are associated with this notion. I believe that therapeutic conversations that are informed by this notion have no bounds. Imagine, for example, further inquiries into the conditions that made it possible for Julie's mother and sister to discern acknowledgement and to attribute it at least some value (this was subsequently taken up in my meetings with Julie and her sister), for the postmaster to discern inclusion and to bring the sort of significance to this that represented it as a special privilege, and for the discernment of injustice expressed by the author of Jane and Sue's book.

I expect that you, the reader, could, at this point, contribute further ideas for therapeutic conversations that are informed by this notion that people's expressions of life are associated with discernments that depend on the absent but implicit. So, it is time for me to now step back.

References

Bateson, G. 1980: *Mind and Nature: A necessary unity*. New York: Bantam Books.

Derrida, J. 1978: *Writing and Difference*. Chicago: University of Chicago Press.

White, M. 1988: 'The process of questioning: A therapy of literary merit.' *Dulwich Centre Newsletter*, Winter.

White, M. 1997: *Narratives of Therapists' Lives*. Adelaide: Dulwich Centre Publications.

White, M. 1999: 'Reflecting-team work as definitional ceremony revisited.' *Gecko*, Vol.2 (reprinted as chapter 4 in this book).

4.

Reflecting-team work as definitional ceremony revisited*

The focus of this essay is the definitional ceremony metaphor and the shape that this gives to reflecting-team work. I have written this to complement two other pieces on this subject (White, 1995, 1997). It is not my intention to reproduce significant aspects of these two pieces here, or to provide a summary of them. Rather, I wanted to write an essay that would complement what I have previously written on this subject, so that the three pieces might be read together.

At the outset of this essay, I discuss the structuralism/poststructuralism distinction. I believe a grasp of this distinction to be essential to an appreciation of the workings of definitional ceremony, and of the contribution of definitional ceremony to identity formation. I then touch on the emphasis that narrative therapy has always given to the identification and recruitment of audiences to the preferred developments of people's lives. Following this, I visit some of Barbara Myerhoff's contributions to an understanding of the workings of definitional ceremony, before further mapping out some of the reflecting team practices that are shaped by this understanding. Last, I focus on some of the

---

* This paper was first published in the 1999, Vol.1 issue of *Gecko: a journal of deconstruction and narrative ideas in therapeutic practice*.

issues that reflecting teams invariably wind up grappling with as they engage with these practices.

TRADITIONS OF THOUGHT AND PRACTICE

The practices of narrative therapy are informed by poststructuralist or non-structuralist understandings of life and of identity. My purpose in emphasising poststructuralist or non-structuralist understandings at the outset of this essay is to call attention to the significance of traditions of thought in regard to implications for therapeutic practice. And I am emphasising this at the outset of this essay about reflecting-team work for several reasons. First, I believe there to be an inseparable link between thought and practice, and not to draw distinctions around different traditions of thought can have the effect of tying us, in the name of therapeutic endeavour, to the unquestioned reproduction of the taken-for-granted and routine habits of thought and action of contemporary western culture. When this is the case, it is more likely that therapy will reinforce the dominant modes of life of this culture, rather than present options that might contribute to the questioning of these modes of life.

Second, I draw this distinction because many of the practices of narrative therapy contrast significantly with the practices of therapy that are derived from structuralist understandings of people's expressions of living. But an appreciation of this is often lost. In this present era the premises of structuralist thought are so spontaneously assumed and so deeply ingrained in the culture of counselling/psychotherapy that many of the proposals for practice that are subsumed under the umbrella of narrative therapy are regularly taken to be a revisioning of the well-known and familiar structuralist ideas and practices – for example, they are often taken to be a recycling of humanist approaches to counselling.

Third, I draw this distinction here because the reflecting-team practices which are the subject of this essay are informed by poststructuralist or non-structuralist understandings of life and of identity. I believe that to discern the structuralist/poststructuralist distinction in the exploration of therapeutic practices, including those of the reflecting team, contributes to an appreciation of the specificity of these practices. This discernment also provides a basis for us to join with each other in the further development of these practices – to extend on the limits of what is known about them.

Structuralist understandings

I believe that it would be helpful to the subsequent discussion of reflecting-team work to take pause to draw out this structuralist/poststructuralist distinction just a little. So, first a word about structuralism. Without doubt, what might be referred to as the 'structuralist project' has been spectacularly successful. After four or five hundred years of development of structuralist understandings of life, structuralist thought is now pervasive in contemporary western culture – so much so, that it has become rather difficult to think of life outside of these understandings.

One characteristic of structuralist thought is the surface/depth contrast. It is within the terms of this contrast that people's expressions of living are taken to be behaviours that are surface manifestations of particular elements or essences. It is generally accepted that these elements or essences can be discovered by plumbing the depths of people's lives. They are envisioned as the building blocks of identity, and are considered to be at what is conceived of as the centre of personhood – a centre that is invariably referred to as the 'self'. In western culture it is now routinely accepted that everybody has one of these 'selves', and it is generally taken for granted that self and identity are inextricably linked – that identity is a product of, or is synonymous with, the self.

What are some of the implications of this structuralist tradition of thought? If the actions and the experiences of people's lives that bring them to counselling/therapy are understood to be expressions that are surface manifestations of deeper 'truths' – for example, of certain elements or essences of a self that is to be found at the centre of identity – then these expressions require expert interpretation. This requirement leads to the production of theories, to the construction of systems of analyses founded on these theories that can be laid over people's lives, and to the development of professional techniques of remediation that will fix whatever it is that is amiss at the centre of their identity.

Poststructuralist understandings

Despite the wide and unquestioned acceptance of the link between identity and self, historians of thought (for example, Michel Foucault), cultural anthropologists (for example, Clifford Geertz), and others from disciplines as apparently disparate as literary theory and science, have drawn attention to the fact that the habit of associating self with identity is a relatively recent phenomenon. But more than this: they have demonstrated the extent to which the idea that there exists such a thing as a 'self', that resides at the centre of personhood, and is a source of meaning and action, is, in the history of the world's cultures, a remarkably novel idea.

Poststructuralist understandings account for identity as a social and public achievement – identity is something that is negotiated within social institutions and within communities of people – and is shaped by historical and cultural forces. In exploring the mechanisms that give rise to identity within these contexts, the structure of narrative frequently comes under scrutiny, for people routinely negotiate meaning within the context of narrative frames – they attribute meaning to their experiences of the events of their lives by locating these in sequences that unfold through time according to certain themes or plots. And more than this: it is in this 'storying' of experience that people derive identity descriptions that are filed into the identity categories of modern culture – motive, need, attributes, traits, properties, and so on. According to this poststructuralist take on life, it is not one's motive that shapes action, but one's account of one's motive that has been socially derived in narrative negotiations that does so.

In comparison to structuralist conceptions of life that are informed by the surface/depth contrast, a characteristic of poststructuralist thought is the contrasting of the metaphors 'thin' and 'thick'[1]. In engaging with this thin/thick contrast, rather than reproducing the time-honoured therapeutic practices of interpreting people's expressions of living through recourse to the expert knowledge discourses of the culture of therapy, and of remedial action on the part of the therapist (which contribute to thin description), the practices of narrative therapy assist people to break from thin conclusions about their lives, about their identities, and about their relationships. But more than this: these narrative practices also provide people with the opportunity to engage in the thick or rich description of their lives, of their identities, and of their relationships. As people become more narratively resourced through the generation of this thick or rich description, they find that they have available to them options for action that would not have otherwise been imaginable.

Some of the practices of narrative therapy that engage with this poststructuralist contrast of thick and thin are shaped by the 'definitional ceremony' metaphor. Definitional ceremony as poststructuralist practice will be the subject of the next section of this essay.

DEFINITIONAL CEREMONY

In the literature on narrative therapy, there can be found various micro-maps for practice that can be taken up as guides in assisting people to break from thin conclusions about their lives and their identities, and that provide options for joining with people in the generation of rich or thick description of these lives and identities (for example, Freedman & Combs, 1996; Zimmerman & Dickerson, 1996; Monk et al., 1997; Freeman et al., 1997; White & Epston, 1991; White, 1995, 1997). In this essay, I will focus on the map that is informed by the 'definitional ceremony' metaphor. The metaphor of definitional ceremony is one that contributes to the structuring of therapy as a context for the telling and the retelling of the stories of people's lives. There is a specificity to these tellings and retellings that constitute definitional ceremonies – it is not a matter of 'anything goes' – some of which I have drawn out in pieces that have been published elsewhere (White, 1995, 1997). It is not my intention here to reproduce the content of these previously published pieces, but to describe some of the particularities of definitional ceremony at work in a way that will complement them.

But first some general observations about the structure of definitional ceremony. The definitional ceremony metaphor guides the structuring of forums in which certain persons have the opportunity to engage in a telling of some of the significant stories of their lives – stories that, in one way or another, are relevant to matters of personal and relational identity. Also present in this forum is an audience or 'outsider-witness' group. The members of this group listen carefully to the stories told, and ready themselves to engage in a retelling of what they have heard. When the time is right, positions are switched – the persons whose lives are at the centre of the definitional ceremony form an audience to the retellings of the outsider-witness group. These retellings encapsulate aspects of the original telling. But more than this – the retellings of the outsider-witness group routinely exceed the boundaries of the original telling in significant ways, in ways that contribute to the rich description of the personal and relational identities of the persons whose lives are at the centre of the ceremony. In part, these retellings achieve this through the linking of the stories of the lives of these persons with the stories of the lives of others, around shared themes, values, purposes and commitments.

After these retellings, the members of the outsider-witness group step back into the audience position, and the persons whose lives are at the centre of the ceremony have the opportunity to speak of what they have heard. At this time these persons are engaged in the second of the retellings; that is, in retellings of the retellings of the outsider-witness group. In these forums, there can be other levels of outsider-witness participation, and further retellings of retellings.

The definitional ceremony metaphor guides the structuring of tellings and retellings of the stories of people's lives in uniquely convened social arenas. Within the context of these ceremonies, these tellings, retellings, and retellings of retellings are distinct. The achievement of these distinct tellings and retellings requires a disruption of dialogue across the interface between those in the audience position and those who are engaged in the tellings and retellings; that is, when the outsider-witness group is in the audience position, they are strictly in that position, and when the persons whose lives are at the centre of definitional ceremonies are in the audience position, they are strictly in that position. Conversation across this interface only occurs at the end of the ceremony, in the fourth and final stage.

There is a specificity to the retellings of the outsider-witness group: in that these retellings contribute very significantly to the rich description of personal and relational identities, they constitute 'regrading' ceremonies of definition. In the usual run of events of everyday life, not all retellings of audience groups achieve this rich description. In fact, many of the institutionalised retellings of the contemporary world contribute significantly to the thin description of personal and relational identity. Consider, for example, many of the routine and taken-for-granted ways of speaking about people's lives in the modern case conference – ways of speaking that are reducing and pathologising of people's lives through processes of normalising judgement. People usually experience a lessening of their identities on account of such retellings. Retellings that contribute to the thin description of personal and relational identities constitute 'degrading' definitional ceremonies.[2]

Audience identification and recruitment

Although this essay has a primary focus on definitional ceremony at work in a relatively specific and formal sense – that is, on definitional ceremony in which the members of the outsider-witness group are drawn from the community of therapists and form a reflecting team – this by no means represents the limits of possibility for work that is shaped by this metaphor. There are countless opportunities available to therapists to engage with this metaphor in the structuring of their work with the people who consult them. The greater majority of these opportunities can be taken up in the convening of relatively informal forums for the telling and retelling of the stories of people's lives.

To this end, over many years, David Epston and I have emphasised the importance of giving attention to the identification and recruitment of appropriate audiences to people's expressions of the significant and preferred developments of their lives. This had been a consistent theme of our own work. We have drawn these audiences from a wide range of contexts – from family and friendship networks, from school and work-place environments, from pools of acquaintances, including neighbours and shopkeepers, and from communities of people who are unknown to the persons who are seeking consultation. A significant source for the identification and recruitment of appropriate audiences is provided by what I refer to as therapists' 'registers'; that is, by lists of people who have previously consulted therapists about a variety of problems and concerns, and who have willingly made themselves available to participate in the structuring of definitional ceremonies for others.

At the end of our consultations with people who consult us, when soliciting reflections on the work that we have done together, we often ask them about their interest in participating, at some future time, in the sort of retellings of the stories of other people's lives that might contribute to the resolution of their problems and concerns. The response to this inquiry has been consistently enthusiastic. At this time, people invariably volunteer to place their names on one of our registers. These registers provide a rich source of people who have insider experience and insider knowledge of the sort of predicaments and concerns over which people seek consultation with therapists.

I want to further emphasise here the importance that we place on the identification and recruitment of these audiences. I am aware that it is often assumed that engaging an audience to people's expressions of the stories of their lives is a relatively peripheral practice of narrative therapy; that giving consideration to the engagement of these audiences is something that is tacked on at the end of the work, as an afterthought; that this engagement is a supplement to the central therapeutic endeavour. This has never been our conception of the status of audience identification and recruitment. This has never been peripheral to our practice. For us, audience engagement has been as much at the centre of our endeavour as have other known narrative practices. I emphasise this here, for in the following discussion I will be mostly focussing on the opportunity that is provided in being able to draw audiences from communities of therapists and/or other related professions. This convening of a reflecting team is an opportunity that is not generally available in the workplace, and I do not want my focus on this relatively restricted version of outsider-witness engagement to contribute to assumptions about this practice having a peripheral status in narrative therapy.

Barbara Myerhoff and Venice, Los Angeles

As previously mentioned, there is a specificity to the outsider-witness group retellings of narrative therapy. Explorations of the sort of retellings that are more likely to contribute to the rich description of personal and relational identities are not informed by the 'anything goes' rule – these retellings of the stories of people's lives are not just *any* retellings. These retellings are not about the evaluation, judgement, or diagnoses of persons' lives through recourse to the expert knowledges of the professional disciplines or according to the premises of popular psychology. These retellings are not shaped by homilies or moral stories derived from the histories of the members of the outsider-witness group. And they are not shaped by the idea of treatment or intervention. Rather, these retellings are the outcome of careful listening and of efforts, on the part of the members of the outsider-witness group, to give expression to particular aspects of the stories heard and to extend on the limits of these stories in ways that are not imposing. In these retellings, the stories of the lives of the people who are at the centre of the definitional ceremony are frequently linked to the stories of the lives of others around shared themes, purposes, commitments and values. A primary mechanism of these retellings is the powerful acknowledgement of people's expressions of their experiences of life. In the therapeutic context, these retellings of the outsider-witness group are usually transformative in their effects.

It is my plan, in this essay, to further describe and illustrate some of the outsider-witness group practices that have been shown, within the context of narrative therapy and reflecting-team work, to contribute significantly to this rich description of personal and relational identities. However, before doing this I will touch on the work of Barbara Myerhoff, as it was through her writings that I first became acquainted with the definitional ceremony metaphor. Myerhoff was a cultural anthropologist whose field work engaged her with a community of elderly Jews in Venice, Los Angeles. Many of the ideas and practices that I discuss in this essay are testimony to Myerhoff's contribution, to the contribution of the people of this community, and to the contribution of Maurie Rosen, an extraordinary community organiser who played such a significant part in assisting the people of this community to breathe life into their identity projects.

Because of considerations of space, my discussion in this section will be brief. However, there are several sources available to readers through which can be gained a greater familiarity with Myerhoff's fieldwork, and with the life of this community (Myerhoff, 1980, 1982, 1986). There is also a documentary film that details some aspects of the of the life of this community and of Myerhoff's fieldwork that is generally available from film libraries. This documentary is called *Number Our Days*, and it won an Academy Award in 1976.

Many of the elderly Jews of the Venice community had migrated from the shtetls of Eastern Europe to North America around the turn of the century.

They had subsequently relocated to Los Angeles in search of a mild climate that would be kind to them in their retirement, and had settled in Venice where relatively inexpensive accommodation could be found. Many of the people of this community had outlived their children, and many had lost their extended families in the Holocaust. For them, isolation and invisibility was a primary threat – the threat of becoming invisible to the wider community, of becoming invisible to each other, and of becoming invisible to themselves to the extent that they would cease to have any sense that they existed at all.

In response to this threat, the members of this community, with great intensity and urgency, instituted and routinely engaged in activities that contributed to the production and reproduction of their own identities. These were not isolated singular and individual activities. Rather, in a multiplicity of ways, they devoted much of their daily lives to shared identity projects. A characteristic feature of these identity projects that caught Myerhoff's attention and captured her imagination was the unique self-reflexive consciousness that was expressed in them. The people of this community expressed a consciousness of their participation in the production of their own and each other's identities – they were conscious of the life-shaping effect of their own contributions to the production of their own lives.

I believe that the self-reflexive consciousness that is a feature of the identity projects of the people of this community reflects a non-structuralist understanding of personhood, and, of course, the Hasidism of their cultural history. This non-structuralist understanding of personhood is evident in the elderly Jews' awareness, lived out in so much of what Myerhoff recounts, of the extent to which one's sense of identity is dependent upon one's engagement with identity projects, and of the extent to which identity is:

a) a public and social achievement, not a private and individual achievement;

b) shaped by historical and cultural forces, rather than by the forces of nature, however nature might be conceived of; and

c) dependent upon deriving a sense of authenticity that is an outcome of social processes that are acknowledging of one's preferred claims about one's identity and about one's history, rather than being the outcome of the identification of, and expression of, the essences or elements of the 'self' through introspection, however that self might be conceived of.

Myerhoff explored, among other things, the structures that the people of this community engaged with in their identity projects. One of these structures she refers to as 'Definitional Ceremony', and she provides an account of how this shaped forums of acknowledgement which were available to the people of this community for the purposes of making personal appearances according to their preferred claims about their identities:

> *When cultures are fragmented and in serious disarray, proper audiences may be hard to find. Natural occasions may not be offered and then they must be artificially invented. I have called such performances "Definitional Ceremonies", understanding them to be collective self-definitions specifically intended to proclaim an interpretation to an audience not otherwise available. The latter must be captured by any means necessary and made to see the truth of the group's history as the members understand it. Socially marginal people, disdained, ignored groups, individuals with what Erving Goffman calls "spoiled identities", regularly seek opportunities to appear before others in the light of their own internally provided interpretation.* (Myerhoff, 1982, p. 105)

It was in these contexts of definitional ceremony that people's identity claims were powerfully acknowledged by the responses of others. It was in these contexts that these identity claims were authenticated by the retellings of the outsider witnesses. It was through this authentication, which is a social process, that an alignment of sense of self and these identity claims was achieved. It was through this social process of authentication that the elderly Jews of Venice were able to achieve the experience of being at one with their identity claims – that they were able to renew their sense of personal authenticity.

In the tellings and retellings of the definitional ceremonies described by Myerhoff, people's lives were 're-membered'. Re-membering refers to a special type of recollection:

> *To signify this special type of recollection, the term 'Re-membering' may be used, calling attention to the reaggregation of members, the figures who belong to one's life story, one's own prior selves, as well as significant others who are part of the story. Re-membering, then, is a purposive, significant unification, quite different from the passive,*

continuous fragmentary flickerings of images and feelings that accompany other activities in the normal flow of consciousness. (1982, p. 111)

As I have discussed this definition of Re-membering, as well as some of the implications of this definition for therapeutic practice, in some detail elsewhere (White, 1995, 1997), I will only touch briefly on this subject here. This definition of Re-membering evokes an image of a person's life and identity as a membered association or club. The membership of this association of life is composed of the significant figures of the person's history, and those figures of the person's contemporary circumstances of life whose voices are influential in regard to matters of the person's identity. Re-membering provides an opportunity for persons to engage in a revision of the membership of their association of life. Myerhoff draws out some of the social mechanisms that contribute to re-membered lives:

Private and collective lives, properly Re-membered, are interpretative. Full or "thick description" is such an analysis. This involves finding linkages between the group's shared, valued beliefs and symbols, and the specific historical events. Particularities are subsumed and equated with grander themes, seen as exemplifying ultimate concerns. (1982, p.111)

Re-membering, according to Myerhoff's definition, contributes to the production of multi-voiced identities. The understanding of identity as a multi-voiced phenomenon is one that contrasts significantly with structuralist understandings that establish identity as a single-voiced phenomenon, as an expression of a self that is to be found at the centre of personhood. Re-membering practices provide for an alternative to the dominant subjectivities of contemporary western culture that are shaped by these structuralist understandings. In this production of multi-voiced subjectivities through Re-membering practices, self and identity cease to be synonymous. Another feature of Re-membering is that it is 'requisite to sense and ordering' in life. It is through re-membering that 'life is given a shape that extends back in the past and forward into the future'.

Myerhoff's contributions to an understanding of the workings of definitional ceremony have substantially influenced my explorations of reflecting-team work. Reflecting-team work as definitional ceremony is the subject of the next section of this essay.

THE REFLECTING TEAM

The reflecting team proposal was first introduced to the family therapy field by Tom Andersen in his 1987 article 'The reflecting team: Dialogue and meta-dialogue in clinical work'. This proposal has been hugely influential since the appearance of this article. It has been taken up into many domains in the family therapy field, and into other fields not just related to therapeutic endeavour, but also to community work and to organisational management. Reflecting-team practices are particularly prevalent in family therapy institutes around the world – these practices have become installed as primary mechanisms for the training of therapists.

Although there are similarities in the structure of the reflecting-team work that is practiced from place to place, today there exists no uniform approach to the emphases, content, themes and styles of team reflections. Neither is there a uniform approach to the relational particularities of reflecting-team work – there are no generally accepted guidelines for team-member participation with each other in the course of their reflections. There is also no consensus in terms of an understanding of the mechanisms at work in reflecting-team work in relation to its frequently transformative effects. I will not attempt here to summarise the multiplicity of approaches to reflecting-team work that have been developed in different contexts and in different locations, nor the various understandings of its workings that have been expressed in the literature. I lack a reasonable degree of familiarity with most of these approaches and understandings, and besides, there are now numerous sources of information available to those who wish to acquaint themselves with a variety of reflecting-team practices (for example, Friedman [ed], 1995, 'The reflecting team in action: Collaborative practice in family therapy'), including this issue of *Gecko*. I will restrict my focus to explorations of reflecting team work that are informed by the definitional ceremony metaphor, and that fit more generally with my engagement with narrative practice.

There are yet further limits to the discussion that follows. I have intended this essay to complement the other pieces that I have previously published on reflecting-team work as definitional ceremony (White, 1991, 1995, 1997). In choosing to complement these other pieces, I have not reproduced here what I have already written about reflecting-team work, but have attended to neglected aspects of this work in response to questions that have been asked of it, and have reiterated other aspects in order to draw these out and to provide greater emphases where I consider this to be important.

Practices of acknowledgement

The outsider-witness retellings of the reflecting-team work of narrative practice contribute significantly to the rich description of personal and relational identities. One of the mechanisms that contributes to this achievement relates to the practices of acknowledgement that are associated with, and that give shape to, these retellings. These practices of acknowledgement are not what they are often taken to be; that is, the contemporary practices of applause – pointing out positives, praising, giving affirmations, providing positive reinforcement, offering congratulations, and so on. This rendering of the contribution of the outsider-witness group is, I believe, an outcome of a very significant narrowing, through recent history, of the regular habits of acknowledgement in our communities. Habits of acknowledgement that are more considered, thoughtful, and more specific in the sense that they are expressed in ways that are unique to the events that they refer to, are increasingly giving way to ready-made and general-purpose responses (which I refer to as the practices of the applause) to the significant events of people's lives.

In including these reflections on practices of acknowledgement, it is not my goal to cast a shadow on the positive intentions or the personal commitment of therapists who participate in reflecting-team contexts in the hope of providing people with healing experiences. Often therapists participating in reflecting teams engage with the practices of applause in their efforts to break from and challenge the routine pathologising of personal and relational identities that is pervasive in the culture of psychotherapy – to break with and to challenge the normalising judgement of people's lives. Pointing out positives, praising, giving affirmation, providing positive reinforcement, and offering congratulations, often seem attractive and ready-made options to this pathologising of people's lives, and furthermore, can easily be read as providing antidotes to this pathologising.

However, these practices of applause do reproduce normalising judgement. For example, congratulatory responses are informed by conclusions that someone has done well by certain measures, and the utterance of such responses is inevitably associated with the assumption that the person expressing congratulations is in a position to make a judgement about another person's performance, and has the means of, or instruments for, assessing this performance. In this critique of the practices of applause – in drawing out the intimate relationship between these practices and normalising judgement – I am not suggesting that the practices of applause do not have a place in everyday life, that these practices inevitably have negative effects, or that there are not occasions upon which their effects are positive.

But in contexts in which there are relatively fixed power relations – as in therapeutic contexts – the normalising judgement that is reproduced through the practices of applause is particularly hazardous. It can contribute significantly to the subjugation of those whose lives are the focus of reflecting-team responses. It can shut the door on the exploration and rich description of knowledges and skills of living that do not fit with the constructed norms of contemporary life. And more than this: expressions of applause can risk alienation – in therapeutic contexts many people experience these practices as patronising, as efforts in persuasion, as reflecting of a lack of general understanding, and as exposing a failure to grasp and to appreciate the circumstances and conditions of their lives.

I believe that engaging with the sort of poststructuralist understandings that I discussed at the outset of this essay can assist reflecting-team members to avoid the reproduction of the practices of applause in the name of acknowledgement. It is with these understandings that team members are more able to stay on track in their intention to participate with each other in contributing to the rich description of the personal and relational identities of the people seeking consultation. When equipped with these understandings of life, team members are better placed to play a significant role in the development of the thick description of the knowledges and skills of living that have been generated in the history of the lives of the persons seeking consultation. It is with these understandings that team members are more able to break from habits of thought and action that encourage them to 'make interventions' into other people's lives. It is through an appreciation of the extent to which a person's identity conclusions are shaped by the stories of their lives, and of the extent to which people live by the stories of their lives, not by the exceptions of their lives, that reflecting-team members are freed from a whole range of considerations. These are considerations that would otherwise make it impossible for them to prioritise being with each other in the generation of retellings of the stories of people's lives that are regrading of their personal and relational identities.

Conversation, not monologue

Just as the outsider-witness practices of definitional ceremony are not a reproduction of the contemporary practices of applause, they are also not a reproduction of the sort of pronouncement about other people's lives that is often present in monologue. Although monologue is not necessarily pronouncement, it always risks pronouncement, even when all intentions and efforts are to the contrary.

To undermine the risk of pronouncement, and to contribute to a context which will be generative of the rich retellings of the stories of people's lives, the outsider-witness practices of reflecting teams engage its members in conversations that evolve over the course of these retellings. This interactive or conversational mode is often shaped by the questions that team members have of each other in response to their different contributions to retellings. Reflecting-team members can set a context for this by reaching some agreement that the act of contributing to retellings signals a preparedness to be interviewed about this contribution by other team members. As part of this agreement, there can also be an understanding that, in response to being interviewed in this way, team members can 'pass' on any questions, or request that these questions be returned to when they have had more time to consider them, or when, for other reasons, they feel more ready to respond to them.

There are many options for the team members to interview each other, and I have detailed some of these options elsewhere. I will not review the scope of these options here, but will again touch on the subject of what I refer to as 'decentred sharing', and emphasise the part that team-member interviewing of each other plays in achieving this.

There are several purposes for engaging in decentred sharing. These do not include purposes like 'self-disclosure', but purposes like 'embodiment' and 'acknowledgement', which I have discussed in 'Reflecting team as definitional ceremony' (White, 1995) and in 'Definitional ceremony' (White, 1997). To embody one's interest in other people's lives is to situate this interest in the context of those people's expressions, in the context of one's own lived experience, in the context of one's imagination and curiosity, or in the context of one's purposes. When one's interest in people's lives is embodied in this way, it is unlikely to be taken as academic or to be experienced as patronising. To embody one's interest in the lives of other people is also to acknowledge the ways in which the expressions of these people have touched one's life, and, more specifically, in the case of outsider-witness practices, to acknowledge the way in which these expressions have contributed to the possibility for becoming other than who one was.

During outsider-witness retellings there is a range of questions that can be asked by team members of each other in their efforts to address this objective of embodiment. For example, team members can ask questions of each other regarding the understandings they have about (a) why their interest has been aroused by particular events of people's lives; (b) what images of people's lives and relationships these events evoke; (c) the sort of identity conclusions that are supported by these images; (d) which of the expressions witnessed are sustaining of these identity conclusions; (e) what these images touch on in the history of their own work and/or of their own lives more generally; and (f) the effects or the potential effects of this 'touching' in regard to the rich description of, and/or possibilities of action in, their own work and lives.

Katharsis revisited

Within the context of definitional ceremony, the retellings of the reflecting team are shaped by an appreciation of the poststructuralist sentiment of contributing to options for people to become 'other than who they were' at the outset of the ceremony, rather than according to a structuralist sentiment that would determine this as a context for people to become 'more truly who they really are'. The extent to which definitional ceremony contributes to options for people to become other than who they were is demonstrated in the extent to which it makes it possible for people to:

a) think outside of what they routinely think, to extend on the limits of their understandings;

b) stand in territories of their lives that are associated with their preferred claims about their identity;

c) experience a multi-layered and multi-voiced sense of identity;

d) engage with knowledges and skills of living that were previously barely traces to be perceived in their histories; and

e) take up options for action in their lives and relationships that would not have otherwise been available or even visible to them.

By this account, it is through engagement in definitional ceremony that people are 'moved'. Here I am using the word moved in a more literal or practice sense than is common. While the expression 'I am moved by this' is usually a signifier that the speaker has had an emotional experience of one sort or another, to be moved in the sense that I am referring to here is the outcome of engaging in a *practice* – it is to engage in practices that have the effect of transporting people elsewhere, and frequently into territories of life and identity in which they could have never been predicted they would find themselves.[3] I referring to the potential of definitional ceremony to move people, I am referring to the members of the reflecting team as much as those whose lives are at the centre of the ceremony. Not only are these definitional ceremonies transporting of persons who are seeking consultation, they are also transporting of the members of the outsider-witness group. As the members of this group come together as an audience to some of the significant stories of people's lives, and actively engage in rich retellings of these stories, they become other than who they were on account of this. It is my understanding that to be moved in the witnessing of expressions of life, in the sense that this is transporting, can be defined as a kathartic experience in a classical sense of this word. And for the members of the outsider-witness group to be together moved in this way evokes

Victor Turner's (1969) 'communitas' – that unique sense of being present to each other in entering liminal circumstances, betwixt and between known worlds.

The contemporary version of catharsis is one of many revisionings, through history, of the classical senses of this word. I believe this revisioning to be linked, in part, to historical developments in both hydraulic and steam-engine technology, and with the associated construction of an 'emotional system' that is informed by these metaphors – the modern emotional system is constructed as a sophisticated part-hydraulic system and part-steam engine in which there are certain pressures to be discharged and energies to be moved, and certain valves to be turned which provide for certain forward movements in life.[4] My preference is to relate to the idea of katharsis in its classical sense – people being moved in the sense of being transported to another place, where they could not have otherwise been, as a result of witnessing a performance of life that is 'gripping' of them.[5] I have consistently found that to evoke katharsis in this classical sense, and within the context of communitas, has been invaluable to team members in orienting themselves as a community of outsider witnesses to the tellings of the stories of people's lives – in their preparation for engaging in outsider-witness retellings, and in their reflections on the constitutive effects of these retellings in regard to their own lives.

Outsider-witness orientation

Earlier in this essay, I touched on the pervasiveness of normalising judgement and its contribution, in therapeutic contexts, to thin conclusions about personal and relational identity. I proposed that poststructuralist understandings of life and of identity provide options for therapists to break from habits of normalising judgement. However, so routine are these habits that the task of breaking from the discourses of normalising judgement can be difficult despite the very best of intentions. For example, as outsider-witnesses to conversations with families, reflecting-team members can find themselves hard-pressed to resist contributing to the construction of 'relational dynamics'.

One antidote to these sorts of structuralist activities is for reflecting teams to engage in explorations of the history of thought and practice in the culture of therapy. In regard to relational dynamics, a historical appreciation would contribute to a questioning of the taken-for-granted status of these 'things' – for example, it would establish the fact that relational dynamics have not been around for all that long, that relationships used not to have these (relationships have only been spoken of in these terms in recent times), and that it has only been over the past few decades that the idea of such 'dynamics' has been popularised. To understand, in this way, that things like relationship dynamics have not always been accepted as fact contributes to options for reflecting-team members to question the unquestioned – for example, to question whether it is a good idea for relationships to have dynamics, to question the real effects of constructing relationships in this way, and to question the place of such constructions in the therapeutic endeavour.

However, achieving a degree of success in the deconstruction of these structuralist understandings can leave therapists facing something of a predicament. So routine is the theorising of life, so accepted is the formal analysis of people's expression of living, and so taken-for-granted are the practices of interpreting the events of people's lives according to the expert knowledge systems of the professional disciplines, that to refuse to participate in this can have the effect of leaving reflecting-team members wondering what is left for them to do. In response to this predicament, in response to a frequently stated desire for structures of listening that might limit engagement with the discourses of normalising judgement, and in response to requests for guidelines about preparing for outsider-witness retellings, I have often proposed that reflecting-team members consider questions such as these:

1. As you listen to the stories of the lives of the people who are at the centre of the definitional ceremony, which of their expressions do you find most gaining of your attention or most capturing of your imagination?

2. How are you to understand the particularities of why it is that your attention is called to the particular expressions that it is called to?

3. What images of people's lives, of their identities, and of the world more generally, are evoked for you by these expressions?

4. In what ways do these images implicate your own life, and in which domains of living do they do this?

5. What reverberations into the history of your own experience are set off by these images? (This can include your personal and relationship history, the historical trajectory of your work, and the history of conversations with the people who consult you.)

6. Are you aware of any events from your own history that are beginning to resonate in relation to these reverberations? If so, what are the specifics of these resonances? What aspects of the history of your experience are these resonances lighting up?

7. In what way are you becoming other than who you were on account of this re-engagement with the history of your own life and work? In what way is this re-engagement contributing to options for action in your life that would not have otherwise occurred to you? How is your participation as a member of the outsider-witness group taking you beyond the limits of what you would routinely think?

8. What are the options for acknowledging this in your contribution to the outsider-witness group retellings that you are soon to participate in?

I provide these questions as a sample of some of the possibilities that are available for reflecting-team member preparation for outsider-witness retellings.[6] They by no means exhaust these possibilities.

Hazards

As with all of the ideas and practices of the culture of therapy, those that I have drawn out in this essay not only bring with them possibilities, but also contribute to limitations and to potential hazards. One of these potential hazards is that reflecting team-members can find their lives thinly described by the persons who are at the centre of the definitional ceremony – team members can experience a lessening of their personhood as a result of people's responses to the outsider-witness retelling, and, needless to say, this is not a good outcome. As contemporary western culture is a culture of normalising judgement, if attention is not given to the potential for people to reproduce these practices of judgement in their responses to the outsider-witness retellings, then team members are engaging in a context that could be significantly disqualifying not just of their efforts, but also of their very personhood.

Before discussing this hazard further, I hasten to draw a distinction between the practices of 'discernment' and the practices of judgement. It is one thing for the people whose lives are at the centre of this work to discern which retellings, or what aspects of any retelling, were helpful and which were either unhelpful or irrelevant to them. It is yet another thing for them to engage in normalising judgement of the performance and identities of the reflecting-team members. While the discernment that I refer to provides an essential guide to the development of relevant and appropriate therapeutic conversations and contributes to a basis for shared research into what it is that constitutes rich description, and what it is that constitutes thin description, it is not helpful for team members to make themselves available to participate in contexts in which they will be subject to normalising judgement.

The people whose lives are at the centre of definitional ceremony are more likely to engage in normalising judgement of, or evaluation of the performance of, reflecting-team members if they live with, and/or have histories of, privilege and advantage. This is particularly so when these people have experienced the privilege and advantage that is associated with high positions in the institutions of our culture, and who experience everyday acknowledgement from those who are in subordinate positions in these institutions. In these observations, I am not casting doubt on the intentions or the integrity of these persons, but calling attention to the contexts that are more favourable to the development of habits of evaluation of the performance of others according to constructed norms – I am calling attention to the situated nature of the acts of normalising judgement of our culture.

There are others who are also prone to reproducing these habits of normalising judgement in definitional ceremony contexts. The lives of these people are often significantly shaped by an ethic of control, and expressions of this ethic are often linked to the power relations of gender. When this is the case, the assumptions of male supremacy and the reproduction of relations of domination are present in men's evaluation of the performance of reflecting teams, particularly in circumstances when the membership of the reflecting team is composed substantially of women.

In response to expressions of normalising judgement that are diminishing of the identities of reflecting-team members, or in those circumstances under which the normalising judgement of the reflecting team is predicted, it is advisable for the interviewer to initiate pre-emptive steps. One option is for the interviewer to institute externalising conversations that encourage explorations of the potential effects of privilege or any of the numerous assumptions of the ethic of control. A preamble to the introduction of these externalising conversations can be helpful, for example:

> *It is not the place of reflecting-team members to engage in acts of judgement of the lives of others. If any of the team members express what I or other team members understand to be statements of judgement, these will be directly questioned in the context of this meeting. After hearing the responses of the reflecting-team members, I plan to consult you about what you have heard, and, as part of this consultation, I will be asking you if you detected any judgement of you as a person. Acts of judgement of the lives of others are quite pervasive. There are also occasions when the people whose lives are at the centre of the retellings of the reflecting team fall prey to habits of judgement in their response to the reflecting team's efforts. When this is the case, it is more difficult for us to understand what is helpful and what is unhelpful about these conversations. And judgement also becomes an obstacle to people hearing what they otherwise might hear, and considering what they would otherwise have the opportunity to consider. So if judgement looks like being an impediment to our work together, I would like to take up the option of discussing this here. Together, then, we might explore the potential effects of this on our work together, and ways of casting it to one side for the duration of our meeting. How does this idea sit with you?*

There are many approaches to this sort of preamble, and some of these can take up the externalising of privilege, advantage, the power relations of local culture (including those of gender), or any of the many assumptions of the ethic of control.

Before moving on to the final topic of this essay, I want to again emphasise the distinction that I have drawn around discernment and judgement. In the third stage of the definitional ceremony, the people whose lives are at the centre of the ceremony are engaged in a retelling of the outsider-witness retellings. At this time, as part of the structuring of this second retelling, these people are consulted about the outsider-witness retellings in a way that solicits the discernment that I have referred to. It is not judgement that is solicited at this time.

Apprehension

It is not unusual for team members to feel a degree of apprehension as they prepare to contribute to outsider-witness retellings. Because apprehension is so often negatively valued in the culture of psychotherapy (for example, the expression of apprehension is sometimes taken by others to reflect a shortfall in the sort of personal confidence that is a requirement of task, or it is read by the person experiencing it as a confirmation of their doubts about their personal competence), it can be helpful to deconstruct this ahead of participation in reflecting-team contexts. It is in conversations that are deconstructing of apprehension that it becomes more richly described. For example, in deconstructing conversations, the expression of apprehension might be understood to be testimony to therapist commitment to modest therapeutic practice in the sea of immodesty that is the culture of therapy; it might be appreciated as a reflection of the sort of deeply ethical position that is the outcome of recognising the responsibility that therapists have regarding the consequences of what they say and do in therapeutic contexts; it might come to represent an acknowledgement of the privilege that is being granted to therapists by the people who are opening their lives to them, and of the gift of trust that these people are investing in these contexts; and so on. It is through the deconstruction of apprehension, rather than through the dishonouring of it, that it ceases to become a major hurdle to the participation of team members in outsider-witness retellings.

It is in training contexts that I regularly join with other therapists in explorations of reflecting-team work that are shaped by the definitional ceremony metaphor. In these contexts, I usually inform therapists that, at the outset of our explorations, some expression of apprehension contributes to my experiencing a degree of confidence that the team's outsider-witness retellings will be regrading of the personal and relational identities of those whose lives are the focus of these retellings. Further to this, at this time it is also my habit to inform therapists that strong expressions of confidence in their ability to engage in outsider-witness retellings that will be of considerable benefit to others makes me acutely apprehensive – I become concerned that I am about to witness a reproduction of some of the practices of immodesty that are relatively commonplace in the culture of therapy.

There are yet other options for addressing team-member apprehension about performance in outsider-witness retellings. In the team's presence, the people whose stories are to be the focus of these retellings can be told that it is not uncommon for there to be hesitation before team members begin to speak of their reflections, and that there may also be some silences along the way. These people can also be informed that this hesitation and any subsequent silence can be taken as an expression of the thoughtfulness of the team members and of their commitment to respond in ways that are not imposing and in ways that might contribute to the opening of new possibilities. In the fourth stage of these ceremonies of definition, reflecting-team members have the opportunity to speak of these hesitations and silences – to speak of the thoughtfulness and to any specific considerations that contributed to the hesitations and silences.

Concluding remarks

In this essay I have revisited reflecting-team work as definitional ceremony. This has provided me with an opportunity to extend on the discussion of some of the ideas and practices of this work, and to emphasise some aspects of it that I consider to have been understated. This revisiting has also given me the opportunity to address some of the frequently asked questions about reflecting-team work as definitional ceremony.

But there is yet more to this story. In describing the mechanisms of definitional ceremony, Barbara Myerhoff includes an account of the performative aspects of the tellings and retellings of the stories of people's lives. And in her account of Re-membering, she describes how 'all the accompanying sensations, emotions, and associations of the first occurrence are recovered and the past recaptured' (1982, p. 109). These performative aspects that are associated with the tellings and retellings of definitional ceremony, and that are highly significant in the outsider-witnesses contributions to thick description, are the subject of a forthcoming essay.

Notes

1. These metaphors are regularly taken up by poststructuralist cultural anthropologists such as Clifford Geertz (1973), Barbara Myerhoff (1982) and Renato Rosaldo (1992). Originally borrowed from Gilbert Ryle, the thin/thick contrast provides a thinking tool for poststructuralist inquiry.
2. For further discussion of this degrading/regrading distinction in regard to social ritual, see Epston (1989).
3. Defining the notion of being 'moved' in this way does not exclude acknowledgement of associated affective experiences, and the accounting of being moved as being transported invariably includes some expression of this associated affective experience.
4. I am grateful to Penny Revel for reminding me that in classical times catharsis was something that was often experienced in the context of community.
5. Modern catharsis is also shaped by the popular and general uptake of the 'confession' into the practices of psychotherapy (Foucault, 1984).
6. I have found Gaston Bachelard's work on the image to be very helpful in reflecting on outsider-witness orientation (1969).

References

Andersen, T. 1987: 'The reflecting team: Dialogue and meta-dialogue in clinical work.' *Family Process,* 26:415-428.

Bachelard, G. 1969: *The Poetics of Space.* Boston: Beacon Press.

Epston, D. 1989: 'Guest Address: Fourth Australian Family Therapy Conference.' In Epston, D., *Collected Papers.* Adelaide: Dulwich Centre Publications.

Freedman, J. & Combs, G. 1996: *Narrative Therapy: The social construction of preferred realities.* New York: Norton.

Freeman, J., Epston, D. & Lobovits, D. 1997: *Playful Approaches to Serious Problems: Narrative therapy with children and their families.* New York: Norton.

Friedman, S. (ed) 1995: *The Reflecting Team in Action: Collaborative practice in family therapy.* New York: Guilford Press.

Foucault, M. 1984: *The History of Sexuality, Volume I.* Great Britain: Peregrine Books.

Geertz, C. 1973: 'Thick description: Toward an interpretive theory of culture.' In C. Geertz (ed), *The Interpretation of Cultures.* New York: Basic Books.

Myerhoff, B. 1980: *Number Our Days.* New York: Simon & Schuster.

Myerhoff, B. 1982: 'Life history among the elderly: Performance, visibility and remembering.' In J. Ruby (ed), *A Crack in the Mirror: Reflexive perspectives in anthropology*. Philadelphia: University of Pennsylvania Press.

Myerhoff, B. 1986: 'Life not death in Venice: Its second life.' In Turner, V. & Bruner, E. (eds), *The Anthropology of Experience*. Chicago: University of Illinois Press.

Monk, G., Winslade, J., Crocket, K. & Epston, D. 1987: *Narrative Therapy in Practice: The archaeology of hope*. San Francisco: Jossey-Bass.

Rosaldo, R. 1992: *Culture and Truth: The remaking of social analysis*. Boston: Beacon Press.

Turner, V. 1969: *The Ritual Process*. New York: Cornell University Press.

White, M. 1991: 'Deconstruction and therapy.' *Dulwich Centre Newsletter*, 3. (Reprinted in Epston, D. & White, M. 1992: *Experience, Contradiction, Narrative & Imagination*. Adelaide: Dulwich Centre Publications.)

White, M. 1995: *Re-authoring Lives: Interviews and essays*. Adelaide: Dulwich Centre Publications.

White, M. 1997: *Narratives of Therapists' Lives*. Adelaide: Dulwich Centre Publications.

White, M. & Epston, D. 1990: *Narrative Means to Therapeutic Ends*. New York: Norton.

Zimmerman, J. & Dickerson, V. 1996: *If Problems Talked: Narrative therapy in action*. New York: Guilford Press.

Interviews

5.

Diversity and narrative therapy

Interviewer: Myrna Gower

Myrna: Your ideas and practices have been influential in many ways and it is difficult now to remember a time when we did not include such ideas in our thinking. If you could only take one or two systemic ideas from the current millennium into the next which would they be?

Michael: Before I respond to this question, I think it might be helpful if I could just clarify my understanding of what it is you are asking. I hope that's okay. When you ask about systemic ideas, I assume that you are referring to family therapy ideas, which are not, by any means, all systemic. Systemic thinking has come to the centre stage at a particular point in the history of family therapy, and this thinking has been highly influential, so much so that the term is regularly present as a preface to, or as a qualifier of, the term family therapy – 'systemic family therapy'.

---

* This interview was first published in *Context: magazine for family therapy and systemic practice*, December 1999, No.46. To subscribe to *Context* please contact Chris Frederick, 12 Mabledon Close, Heald Green, Cheadle, Cheshire SK8 3DB, UK. Ph/fax: (44-161) 493 9012.

** Myrna Gower is a member of the editorial group of *Context: magazine for family therapy and systemic practice*.

In other situations (such as within the subtitle of *Context: A magazine for Family Therapy and Systemic Practice*) it is still possible on the one hand to recognise the specificity of systemic thinking and its proposals for practice, and on the other hand to acknowledge family therapy as an endeavour that relates to some broad themes that can be traced through many of the 'schools' or traditions of family therapy thought and practice, many of which do not conceive of the family as 'a system'.

Myrna: How would you define these themes that inform what you consider to be the endeavour of family therapy?

Michael: One theme is evident in the persistent efforts of family therapists to contribute to an understanding of people's problems within terms of the wider contexts of life: for example, within the family; within many other institutions of society; within the power relations of local culture; within accustomed ways of speaking about and thinking about life, and so on.

Another theme is characterised by a questioning of the taken-for-granted idea of our modern times that people's identities are principally a manifestation of a self that is considered to be at the centre of who we are, and, instead, by a joining with people in explorations of the ways that identity is constituted in family relations – whether this be family of origin, family of imposition, or family of choice – and through history and culture. Associated with this theme then, is a general rejection of essentialist notions of identity formation.

A third theme can be witnessed in a commitment to an interactional or participatory approach to addressing these problems, through meeting with families and other communities of people, and in the emphasis that is given to a focus on the negotiation and renegotiation of people's identities within this interactional or participatory approach.

I should add here that, in these efforts to address problems and in this negotiation and renegotiation of identity, I do not believe that all material engagements with the significant figures of people's lives have to occur within the therapist's office in order for these common themes to be reproduced in family therapy practice.

Myrna: So, these are the primary themes that you see linking of the work of many family therapists of different persuasions?

Michael: I am sure that the themes that I draw here that link together many therapists who relate to 'family therapy' could be better drawn, and I also have no doubt that others would have different understandings. But I believe that it is a worthwhile endeavour to work to identify such themes.

The identification of themes like these could invite an engagement with the history of the endeavour of family therapy in ways that would make possible the acknowledgement of different traditions of thought and practice that dot the historical landscape of this endeavour.

In no way am I suggesting this acknowledgement of difference in order to disqualify systems ideas and the practices associated with this. Much of that which is informed by the systems metaphor addresses the themes of family therapy I just described. I am simply suggesting that it is not at all necessary to engage with the systems metaphor to continue what I understand to be the endeavour of family therapy. Some of the other traditions of thought and practice that do take in the themes I described above are not only discontinuous with the thought and practice associated with the systems metaphor, but, in fact, explicitly refute the systems metaphor. Perhaps the new millennium could be a time of both acknowledging the histories of these themes and also the different ways family therapists of many persuasions are currently engaging with them.

So, finally, in response to your initial question (!), I will continue to explore yet other ways of engaging with the themes that I understand to be characteristic of the family therapy endeavour into the next millennium in my meetings with people who live together, who play together, and who struggle with each other. These themes I understand to be the best part of a tradition of family therapy that now has a fifty year history, which I am grateful for.

Myrna: Which of the ideas in the therapy will you be happy to leave behind?

Michael: In speaking of these themes and of the tradition of family therapy as I have, I am not wearing rose-coloured glasses. There is much to be left behind. But this is the case in every field of inquiry. It goes without saying that we regularly think within the terms of what is routinely thought in the time/era and in the place in which we are located in culture. And at times, in special circumstances, we are able to identify some of these limits in regard to thought, and to think past what we routinely think. This opens new options for action in the world. This is what many of the pioneers of family therapy did – in some ways they thought beyond what was routinely thought at the time that they thought this. This was their contribution, their legacy. But, this thinking beyond is fragmentary, and there are always so many perimeters of thought that we are unable to identify and that we cannot shift. So it is inevitable that in our ideas and in our work with families we will be always be reproducing of taken-for-granted ways of thinking and acting, aspects of which, with the benefit of the sort of hindsight that becomes available through being at another place and time in culture, we might be able to question, to challenge, and have the option of leaving behind. This doesn't mean that things new are good and things old are not good, or that we must engage in an effort to leave anything behind. Rather, it suggests that we can look forward to developments that will provide yet further bases for the appraisal of aspects of what it is that goes in the name of family therapy.

Myrna: So, how are these considerations relevant to the teaching/learning context?

Michael: I believe that these observations hold for ideas about training as much as they do for ideas about family therapy. There is already much that has been left behind. And there is also much that has, so far at least, stood the test of time – like the principle of the direct observation of the interviews of people in training, the use of teams in this context, the emphasis on the development of specific skills, and so on.

Myrna: What do you see as being left behind?

Michael: One thing that is being left behind is the centring of the trainer in the training process. Of course, in this development, trainers still provide a frame and work to invite those in training to open space to step into this frame in order to play with specific ideas and practices that are delineated by it. But less and less are these contexts for the imposition of ideas and practices. More and more we are seeing the development of a sensitivity, on behalf of trainers, to the

Diversity and narrative therapy 93

specifics of why it is that certain ideas and practices are more relevant to the people in training than other ideas and practices. And more and more trainers are attending to what it is about the lived experiences of those in training that links them to these ideas and practices, and to how this might be more fully expressed in their work with the people who consult them.

Myrna: Could you name an important change that you think family therapy training programmes will have to make to adjust to the demands of the next millennium?

Michael: In terms of developments in family therapy in general, I think that we will see fewer theory-led initiatives, and more initiatives that are informed by the families and by other groups of people who seek our consultation. In contributing to a climate of this sort, I believe that the emphasis in family therapy training will be on the further development of practices that are effective in contributing to the identification of the 'insider' knowledges of the people in these families and communities, and on the further development of skills in joining with people in their efforts to put these insider knowledges more fully into expression, not just in addressing the problems for which they seek therapy, but in changing local culture.

Myrna: We know that your training programmes have expanded to include a trainee population from the wider community – managers, the business community, witnesses who share interests and larger political systems. Do you think this is likely to become the direction of training development and that clinical family therapy training as we know it, will become obsolete?

Michael: I don't believe that what you are referring to as clinical training in family therapy will ever become obsolete. As we see yet further challenges to the grand narratives of human development, and to the programs for people's lives that are associated with these grand narratives, I believe that there is a chance that we might also witness the fashioning of a more experimental culture. If this is so, there will be increased attention given to forms of inquiry about life that give rise to possibilities for it to become other than what it is, when these other forms cannot be known or specified in advance. In these circumstances the practices and skills that I have already alluded to in this interview could be much in demand.

Myrna: In the new Millennium, what will your writing be about? What might be their titles?

Michael: I don't know, but I am looking forward to finding out. I don't even know what I will be teaching next year, and I hope that I find this out sooner rather than later!

Myrna: From what we read and hear, the splits evolving between narrative and systemic therapies seem to be widening. Is that your personal experience and could you say what you see to be the main implications of this for your training institute?

Michael: From what I read and hear, this does seem to be the general impression out there in the family therapy world. But again, if, when you say systemic therapies you are referring to family therapy generally, this is not the case for me. I don't find this split in my practice – I meet with lots of families. Nor do I find this to be the case generally in my connection with the 'field' – I have strong, loving and respectful connections with many family therapists of different persuasions.

If you are specifically referring to systems therapy, this impression of an evolving split suggests that there was a time in recent history at which people engaging with narrative ideas and those engaging with the systems metaphor were more in accord than they are at this present time. This may well be the case for some, but again, this is not so for me. There is no split widening because there has never been anything to be widened, or, for that matter, to be narrowed. Perhaps I can illustrate this by giving brief mention of my contact with Gianfranco Cecchin, whose name is invariably connected to 'systems thinking'. I have many fond memories of conversations with Gianfranco Cecchin over the years about some of the significant distinctions present in the different traditions of thought that are associated with the systems metaphor and with narrative ideas, and about the different implications for practice that are connected with these ideas. Although most of these conversations have been informal, about ten years ago, or more, we joined with each other in conducting a workshop on this subject in Calgary, one that was coordinated by Karl Tomm. In all of these conversations, we have never reached agreement on these matters, and I don't believe that such an achievement as this has ever been on the agenda for either of us. Rather, these conversations have been challenging – and they have also had the effect of confirming differences and, as well, shared understandings. There is no split that has widened or narrowed over this time.

Myrna: Do you still see Gianfranco as you go about your travels?

Michael: I do lament the fact that Gianfranco Cecchin and I have not crossed paths much in recent years – I have missed him. This is not a reflection of the presence of a split of the sort you have referred to, but of the fact that, because of the quirks of scheduling, we just haven't been able to be at the same events. In all of my contacts with Gianfranco Cecchin and Luigi Boscolo, who, along with Mara Selvini and Guliana Prata figure prominently for their contribution to thinking past the limits of what has been routinely thought in this field, I have experienced a graciousness and a spirit of generosity with which they have welcomed me and included me. I very much look forward to the next time our schedules correspond. This is something I am confident of predicting will occur in the next Millennium!

So, in relation to these impressions of an increasing split between narrative therapists and systemic therapists, as you asked of my personal experience, I have tried to restrict my response to this – and in my personal experience there is no evolving division. There are, of course, conversations that others are engaging in with regard to these issues. Perhaps at another time I could speak of some of my understandings of what is occurring in these conversations that could be contributing to others' experiencing such a split.

Myrna: One last question. As we come to the end of the millennium are there any particular hopes you have for the future in relation to the family therapy field?

Michael: Yes. I hope that *Context* continues to publish in the spirit in which it has in this present millennium. It is one of my favourite reads!

6.

Direction and discovery:
A conversation about power and politics in narrative therapy*

Michael White, Michael F. Hoyt** & Jeff Zimmerman***

Michael H: I'd like to begin by asking you to reflect on how to balance the ideas of direction and discovery. How do you balance the idea that on the one hand the therapist isn't in charge, is de-centred, but, on the other hand is still responsible and is actively doing something in therapy? I'm interested in how this is different than having some sort of treatment plan and trying to march the client to a certain place. What do you listen for? Is there a way to listen so you're participating but not leading? Or are you leading?

---

* The following edited discussion took place on March 16, 1998, in Cupertino, California. Michael White had just completed the first half of a two-day workshop on 'Re-membering, definitional ceremony, and rich description'

** Michael Hoyt is a California-based psychologist. He is the author of *Brief Therapy and Managed Care* (1995), and *Some Stories are Better than Others* (2000); editor of *Constructive Therapies*, Vol.1 & 2 (1994, 1996), and *The Handbook of Constructive Therapies* (1998); and the co-editor of *The First Session in Brief Therapy* (1992).

*** Jeffrey Zimmerman is Director of the Bay Area Family Therapy Associates in Cupertino, California. He is a co-author with Vicki Dickerson of *If Problems Talked: Narrative Therapy in Action* (1996).

Michael W: We're certainly playing a part that is directive in terms of what gets taken up, from these conversations, for further exploration. We do play a significantly directive role in that. But that's not to say that we are directing things in the sense that we are authoring the actual accounts of people's lives that are expressed in these conversations. In all of these conversations we do hear, in people's stories, a whole range of expressions that provide points of entry to different accounts of their lives. Take the videotape of Alice (Alice, a woman who had been consistently subject to abuse in her childhood and adolescence, had appeared in a videotape that was shown in the workshop). In these conversations we hear certain expressions that draw our attention to knowledges of life and skills of living that can be relatively invisible to the people who consult us, and the recognition of these knowledges of life and skills of living shapes our responses in these conversations. So, it is the case that we will be playing a part in the identification and in the rich description of these other knowledges and skills of living, but we don't radically construct these. In reflecting on how Alice began to describe these knowledges and skills, and on her unique naming of them, I believe that it is quite evident that this is not something that I could have come up with. The whole of her account of her 'passion for justice', including the history of this as a theme in her life, and the ways that this has sustained her through all of the trauma that she had been subject to, was built in a context that presented Alice with options for a re-engagement with her own life. This account of Alice's life, including the general naming of it as 'passion for justice', and the identification of the particularities of her life that constitute this theme, is not one that I could have independently or substantially authored.

Jeff: In some ways I suppose we direct a certain kind of discovery. We direct a kind of conversation that constructs contexts which invite certain kinds of discoveries to be made. I certainly feel like I'm doing much better work when I'm thinking in terms of discovery than when I'm orientated towards being directive. Personally, I find it easier to remain in this discovery–mode when working with children. At times with adults I can waver towards the directing end and I don't like the effects this can have.

Michael W: I think that we are all capable of being directive at times. There are all sorts of ways that we can be engaged in practices that take us away from what Jeff is calling 'discovery'. Perhaps some consciousness of this is a partial remedy as it can assist us to avoid engaging in therapy in a way that simply contributes to a confirmation of what we, as therapists, already know. The confirmation of the known is what can take place in the name of therapy. And conversations that just contribute to a confirmation of the known are often dead-ended conversations.

Michael H: How is it that you stay in touch with the person's agenda for seeking consultation in the first place?

Michael W: People's agenda for these conversations frequently change as the conversations develop. So often people change what they want in life as these conversations progress. They might start with a highly specific agenda, and although at times this endures, usually there is some modification in this. As these conversations make it possible for people to stand in different territories of their lives, territories that differently construct their identities and in which different knowledges and skills of living become available for exploration, they identify other purposes for the therapeutic conversation.

Michael H: These orientations to therapy conversations that you are talking about, how do they relate to post-structuralist inquiry? It would seem to me that there is significant difference between asking questions in the hope of getting to a particular place, and asking questions to which you genuinely do not know where the answers will lead ...

Michael W: I think that engaging in some explicit challenge to structuralist conceptions of life is helpful in relation to this. If there is nowhere particular to arrive at, no previously established destinations that are granted some normative or 'truth' status, then there are many possibilities for us to speak about things that we have never spoken about, and to journey to places that we could never have predicted journeying to.

Jeff: I find the distinction of coming from a place of curiosity, rather than a place of 'I'm going to build a landscape' a helpful one. If I can follow the client's experience and stay curious in relation to it, I feel I'm doing good work.

Michael H: Let me read you two quotations and then ask your reflections. They are both related to this consideration of the balance between direction and discovery. The first comes from the *Newsweek* article featuring narrative therapy when David Epston said: 'Every time we ask a question we're generating a possible version of a life' (Cowley & Springen, 1995). The second is from an interview that Salvador Minuchin did within the *Family Therapy Networker*, he was quoted:

> *I remember seeing Michael White do a very masterful session of narrative therapy, but it was like watching a sheep dog at work. He kept pushing people through a series of constructed questions into the groove of seeing their stories in the more positive way that he wanted for them. The therapist changes the old story and convinces the client that the new story is more true than the old. We all offer our patients a language, and we say, 'Let's begin to see your life in this language, and I will give you solutions in this language'. I do it. Everybody does it.* (in Simon, 1996, pp. 55-56)

What do you think of these two characterisations?

Michael W: I have always admired Minuchin's questioning of therapeutic practices, and his efforts to encourage people to acknowledge and to name the power relations of therapy. And, although I don't see myself or my work in the description of Minuchin's that you quoted, I think the issue of the role and meaning of questions in therapeutic conversations is a really good one to consider. I am interested in how we can talk about this issue in ways that do not blur distinctions around different practices. This is important because if all acts of power in the name of therapy are equal – if it is not possible to differentiate between those acts that are more imposing from those that are less imposing – then we don't have anywhere to go in terms of questioning therapeutic practice, and there will be no impetus for us to find ways of making what we do more accountable to the people who consult us.

So, let's talk about the meaning and role of questions within narrative therapy. We could start by considering the context of David Epston's comment

Direction and discovery

that you quoted: 'Every time we ask a question we're generating a possible version of life'. I believe that here David is referring to the fact that a well-formed narrative question can be highly evocative of alternative images of a person's identity. But David is not referring to the sort of questions that are imposed from out of the blue. Rather, he is referring to questions that are formed by therapists in response to people's expressions. How do these questions generate a possible version of life? These images often generate reverberations that reach down through a person's history, reverberations that touch on historical experiences, that set off resonances. Suddenly the person finds themself speaking of some of their experiences of the events of their life that line up with and that support the image that was evoked by the question. At times these are experiences of events of life that the person has never previously given voice to. In regard to developing an understanding of this process, I have found Gaston Bachelard's work on the image to be quite helpful (Bachelard, 1969).

Michael H: Elsewhere Minuchin made another statement in relation to control within therapy conversations.

Control does not disappear from family therapy when it is re-named 'co-creation'. All that happens is that the influence of the therapist on the family is made invisible. Safely underground, it may remain unexamined ... The bottom line is that the constructivist approach, by bracketing the idiosyncratic story, obscures the social fabric that also constructs it. [pp.7-8] ... Constructivist practice, with some exceptions, robs the therapist of human complexity. (1992, p. 10)

Michael W: I think it would be fair to say that Minuchin and I share an interest in exploring the practices of power involved in therapeutic conversations. Minuchin says some things here that I agree with. I have heard accounts given of a practice that is referred to as 'constructivist' practice that does appear to obscure the power relations of therapy and what he refers to as the social fabric. To deny the power relations of therapy in this way makes the therapist less accountable for exercises of power and for the real effects of this in the shaping of people's lives. And to obscure 'social fabric' that shapes the stories of people's lives would surely contribute to a personal burden. So, what Minuchin is saying here really strikes a chord for me. I would agree with his comments on the therapeutic practices that he *calls* 'constructivist' – I emphasise calls here, because I don't know whether or not 'constructivists', whomever they might be, would agree that Minuchin is reasonably representing their position on these matters. Like Minuchin, I would be interested in the responses of constructivist thinkers to these important questions about power and about the social fabric.

Jeff: I notice that you are quite particular in identifying different traditions of thought and how they influence therapeutic practice.

Michael W: Well yes, I believe that this is important. In this quote of Minuchin's, for example, I don't take his comments to be a critique of poststructuralist informed practices as I know them. I have never considered what I think and what I do to be 'constructivist'. I don't have much familiarity with constructivism, and I don't have an appreciation of the history of this tradition of thought. I am not suggesting that Minuchin is representing as constructivist the sort of post-structuralist inquiry that shapes narrative explorations, but it is not unusual these days to see different traditions of thought and practice collapsed on to each other in ways that actually obscure what is being proposed in each of these distinct traditions. For example, in the literature I have read accounts of my thought and practices that represent me as an 'anti-realist', despite the fact that I have little sympathy for what is proposed in this tradition, and despite the fact that I believe the realist/anti-realist debate to be irrelevant to what I know of poststructuralist inquiry and narrative practice. I have also been represented as a social constructionist and a postmodernist. While I can relate to and appreciate many of the ideas that are represented as social constructionist, in this tradition of thought there is also much that leaves me unsatisfied. And I know just little fragments of the specificity of postmodernism, which has its roots in art and literature. Perhaps this specificity is now becoming lost, as the term postmodernism is now often employed to categorise any idea and practice that does not reproduce foundationalist thought. But even the specificity of this description is at risk. I have recently seen postmodernism represented as a form of 'anything goes' moral relativism, as the achievement of simultaneously holding multiple beliefs or views or theories about life, and even as a 'new eclecticism'. I think that this is an unfortunate turn, because in it postmodernism has come to represent what it contradicts.

On any account, this running together of distinct traditions of thought and practice is unhelpful. It leads to the false representation of the position of different thinkers. It destroys a climate of thought by manufacturing a soup that is so thick that it is indigestible, and one in which the different flavours can no longer be distinguished. As an outcome, discerning action in the name of therapy becomes impossible. And therapists are deprived of any clarity in regard to the development of proposals for the further exploration of specific ideas and practices.

It can also become quite amusing! Sometimes, because of the blurring of distinct traditions of thinking, it is claimed that, in what I have written about what I think and do, I haven't properly acknowledged certain thinkers. Simultaneously, it is sometimes said that if I did acknowledge these thinkers then I wouldn't have written what I have written about what I think and do because I wouldn't then think these ways and do these things in the way that I do them!

Michael H: And you believe that conundrums of this sort are the product of this blurring of different and distinct traditions of thought?

Michael W: Often this seems to be the case. At times even the poststructuralist informed proposals of narrative practice are run together with those that are based on linguistic analyses which are informed by structuralist ideas. I believe that to question this lumping together of these different traditions, and to untangle these, is important, as it makes it more possible for all of us to see a way ahead, irrespective of our persuasions.

I think it's really important that the distinctions remain clear, and that yet more of these be drawn. For these distinctions to be blurred makes it very difficult for therapists in our field to experience a degree of conscious choice in terms of the ideas and practices that they wish to engage with, and to reflect on these ideas and practices as they monitor the effects of these in their work with people who seek consultation. Also, when these distinctions are blurred we cannot find a place in which we might sit together, regardless of our differing persuasions, and engage in conversations with each other in which we might all extend on the limits of what we already think.

Jeff: I would be interested in how we can have these conversations. Especially as when we view the work of others, from an outsiders perspective, what we see is often quite different from that which is seen by those who are actually practicing it. For example, I am sure that my view of structural therapy from an outsider's perspective is quite different from those who are structural therapists. We bring our own interpretations and understandings. Finding ways to make further distinctions between certain practices I think would be very helpful.

Michael H: In terms of making these sorts of distinctions, I want to ask you Michael an historical kind of question. I read some of your earlier papers. At some time you were writing more in a cybernetics and strategic frame. What do you think you gained in the shift?

Michael W: I have gone through different phases in my explorations, and in these phases I have framed my work in various ways, including in the ways that are informed by the some of the schools of family therapy. Several experiences assisted me to break from some of these efforts. And some of these breaks were in the form of a U-turn. For example, in the latter part of the seventies, Cheryl White expressed concerns about the direction of my explorations in therapy – that these were engaging me in relational politics that were taking me away from my preferred values and preferred ways of being in my life, and limiting of my considerations of the power relations of local culture, including those considerations shaped by some appreciation of a feminist consciousness, one that Cheryl had introduced me to in the first place at the beginning of the seventies. So, Cheryl's expression of these concerns, her identification of and naming of them, and her faith in the fact that I could find another way, was instrumental in my return to the spirit of my earlier engagement with therapeutic practice.

And there were many singular events that were significant. For example, around 1980 I sent Eleanor Werthiem a manuscript that I had been working on, and soon after had the pleasure of meeting her on a visit to Melbourne. She said that she appreciated those parts of the manuscript that provided an account of what actually happened in my therapeutic conversations with families of young children, but confronted me on my attempts to formalise an understanding of this by engaging with theory. Eleanor's challenge to me was powerful and direct. She chose her words carefully, and they kept ringing in my ears for quite some time.

There have been, of course, many other influences upon the directions I have taken in my explorations. But the influence of Cheryl White, and some encounters with people like Eleanor Werthiem, were particularly significant.

Michael H: This reminds me of passage written by Lynn Hoffman (1993). She wrote:

> *I became particularly aware [in the early 1980s] of the unconscious sexism of all styles of family therapy. Up to that time, most family therapists had accepted them without question. Even when colleagues of mine applied feminist principles to their practice, they focused upon particular injustices like mother-bashing but did not question very much the models they had been trained in. Mainly pioneered by men, these styles went from benign paternalism to an extreme focus on hierarchy, secrecy and control. Even feminist versions kept therapists in a power position in relation to the people the therapists saw. How else could they 'empower' them? I began to ask questions ... To become an another activist seemed too close to becoming another kind of expert, so for the moment I stayed quiet on the subject. I still continued to search for less hierarchically organised family therapy that would enlarge the options for all.*

Do you have any thoughts about this?

Michael W: I know that Lynn Hoffman has made a very significant contribution towards this search for less hierarchically organised family therapy – in fact a very significant contribution to many explorations of a whole range of questions in this field. And, as well, Lynn, along with other feminist family therapists, has raised the relations of gender and power within therapeutic conversations. I believe that this has made very real differences to the ways in which family therapy is practiced.

Michael H: I know that the works of certain anthropologists have been influential in your work. For instance in deconstruction and therapy you quoted Clifford Geertz:

> *The wrenching question, sour and disabused, that Lionel Trilling somewhere quotes an eighteenth-century aesthetician as asking - - 'How Comes it that we all start out Originals and End up Copies?' - - Finds ... an answer that is surprisingly reassuring: it is the copying that originates.* (1986)

How do you understand this?

Michael W: It is a lament that very much speaks to a humanist essentialism, one that asserts the existence of certain elements and substances that make up a self that is at the centre of who we. It is a lament that takes for granted not only the existence of this self, but that there is a 'truth' of human nature to be found in these essences, and that this represents what is 'original' about being human. What is lamented is that this original is lost to processes of socialisation and enculturation, to the forces of repression. There are many contemporary versions of this lament, and, in the culture of therapy, these inspire the development of practices that supposedly assist people to become more truly who they really are by challenging whatever it is that is considered to be repressive and by 'liberating' what it is that is deemed to be original about the self – so that a life can be more exactly and expression of these essences.

Clifford Geertz is a cultural anthropologist who has a non-essentialist understanding of identity formation. Non-essentialist understandings are a challenge to the modern idea that there is a self that is at the centre of who we are. Geertz would have us invert this lament that we have been speaking of, and in this inversion it is recast as: 'How Comes It that we all start out Copies and End up Originals?' This turns out to be a far more interesting question, one that breaks us from naturalistic accounts of identity. It is a question to which Geertz responds: 'It is the copying that originates'. In this sense, rather than to become more truly who we really are, 'originating' refers to the identity-shaping activity that contributes to us becoming other than who we were.

To invert this lament engages us in a fascination with the specificity of and consequences of people's acts of living as they go about reproducing the stories of their lives, as they go about the social negotiation and renegotiation of accounts of their identity. It draws our attention to people's self-shaping activities: to the extent to which people's responses to the contingencies of their lives takes them past the previously known limits of their existence; to the way that people's efforts in maintaining coherent expressions of their identity as they navigate through the different contexts of their lives contributes to revisions in their accounts of and experience of this very identity; to how people's management of the predicaments, dilemmas and contradictions of their lives contribute to possibilities for them to think outside of what they would have otherwise thought, and so on. To engage with the inverted version of this lament centres meaning-making as an achievement that is constitutive of life. In their attempts to reproduce identity in acts of living, people wind up originating – the reproduction of identity encapsulates the copy that went before, but it is more than that.

Jeff: What I want to comment on is the real effects of Geertz's construction. For me, the effect of reversing this lament is to take all the pressure off. If there is no person or thing I'm supposed to live up to, to be compared against, even if I'm attempting to copy or working in a similar way then I am freed from the sort of judgement based on some imagined 'hard' criteria. I am freed up to celebrate differences.

Michael H: Do you mind if I shift the direction a bit and ask a different question? Let me frame it as a quotation from something you said in an earlier conversation, Michael in relation to transference and technologies of power:

> *But these technologies of transference are not just the historical conditions for the constitution of the transference phenomenon. Transference can also be read as the 'trace' of very present power relations ... So, a strong and ongoing experience of transference can cue people to the fact that they are in a subject position in an inflexible power relationship that could lead to domination. This reading of transference opens possibilities for action that can include a refusal of this power relation.*
>
> *I don't want to be misrepresented on this point. I'm not saying that there is no such phenomenon as transference. And I do understand that*

there are those who would justify bringing forth this phenomenon with the idea that this establishes a context for working through issues of personal authority, and so on. But I do think that there is a politics associated with this phenomenon, and [I] would raise questions about the deliberate and not so deliberate reproduction of these politics in the therapeutic context. And I would also want to explore the sort of questions that could contribute to a dismantling of the therapeutic structures that reproduce this phenomenon. (White in Hoyt & Combs, 1996, p. 50)

So, how do you see the politics associated with this phenomenon? And what questions would you raise about it?

Michael W: If someone experiences transference in relation to me, then I want to understand in what ways I might be complicit in the reproduction of certain power relations. I want to explore how we can establish a therapeutic context that contributes to an awareness of the contribution I might be making, wittingly or unwittingly, in the reproduction of power relations that could drift towards relations of domination. It may be that I am speaking with taken-for-granted privilege and that I'm not aware of this. It may be the way that I sit or generally arrange my body in space that is an expression of the power relations of gender. Whatever. I am interested in the options available for rendering more visible these sort of practices of power, as well as the real and potential effects of these, so that they can, to some extent at least, become available to us to modify. What are your thoughts about this?

Jeff: I'm interested in how de-centering practices can assist in reducing the chances of what is known as transference. I guess I'm also curious about the effect of the stories that people might bring with them about the counselling process and what a difference this can also make.

Michael W: And it's not just certain people's private stories either. In seeking therapy people often come to an office which is a formal space in which the therapist's authority is assumed. There are many factors which contribute to the sort of power relations than can create a context for what is known as transference.

Direction and discovery 109

Michael H: Perhaps particularly with a male therapist and a female client, it's all too easy to fall into a reproduction of stereotypic gender politics. This potential reproduction also exists in doing therapy with persons who have been subject to sexual abuse as Rachel Hare-Mustin has written about (1992, 1994).

Michael W: Rachel Hare-Mustin has had, and continues to have, a very significant and eloquent voice in this field on the power relations of local culture, including on the power relations of gender in therapy. She consistently works to encourage this therapy field to acknowledge these power relations and to prioritise them in considerations of therapeutic practice.

Michael H: You have also spoken and written about the importance of making this a priority.

Michael W: I have written about the potential for the inherent power differential within the therapeutic context to have negative effects on the lives of those who have survived abuse and about some of the practices of accountability that are possible for male therapists to engage with when working in these contexts (1995). I believe these are very relevant and significant concerns.

It is also possible for us to engage with other practices of accountability throughout all therapeutic conversations. For example, there are questions we can ask that might reduce the potential for the sort of power relations that we are talking about to become toxic in their effects. We can routinely consult people about the direction of the therapeutic conversation:

- *How is this conversation going for you?*
- *Are we talking about what is important for us to be talking about, or are we off track in this?*
- *How does this conversation fit with the agenda that you came here with?*
- *Would you catch me up with how this conversation is going for you. This will help us to figure out where to go next.*
- *It seems to me that we are at a point where there are a number of possible directions for our conversations. These would all take us into different explorations of your life and relationships. I would like to share my thoughts*

about these possibilities with you, and then consult you about a couple of things: other ideas that you might have for the direction of our conversation, and which of all of these possibilities most interest you.

Apart from all else, consultations of this sort make it clear that the therapist can't assume to know what might be the relevant and appropriate conversations to be having with others, and that she or he is not an authority on what is best for others.

Jeff: I absolutely agree, and this takes me back to the conversation about transference. If I think back to the couple of times that I have had the experience of transference happening, I would see myself as 100% complicit in it. In deconstructing what had occurred I would have seen that I had positioned myself in a way in which I placed myself in a position of power, or one of monitoring the experience of those who had come to consult with me. I think it would be interesting to consider what are the practices of therapy and therapists that construct the phenomenon of transference.

Michael H: As a part of deconstructing these practices I'd be interested in how therapists can proceed so as to learn about and from the people consulting us rather than appearing to be 'assessing' them or checking them out. How can we ensure that we are not engaging in 'grading' these people?

Michael W: I'm really interested in what you are saying. We have a culture of evaluation. These times could be called the 'grading times'. This is the 'rating-table' era. Our present era is the era of the developmental continuum. When we trace the history of this culture of evaluation we can see how modern processes of the judgement of people's actions are intimately associated with, and in the service of, reproducing our society's constructed norms.

Even just norms for living. Modern systems of power engage people in disciplines of the self. It is through the disciplining of the self that people might close the gap between where they stand and the constructed norms of our culture. It is through the sort of practices of evaluation and grading that you speak of that therapists can become agents of this disciplinary technology.

Jeff: I notice that I do this. We all do this. Today I recall in the workshop you

Direction and discovery

said to someone, 'That was a good question.' There are practices like that which we say out of habit without reflection which inadvertently represent grading or evaluation. What I sensed you really meant was 'that's interesting to me' or something like that.

Michael W: Yes, it's certainly a different response, to say: 'That is very interesting to me as well', or 'That captures my imagination too'.

Michael H: Positive affirmations, although well-intended, still serve to maintain the idea of performance evaluation. It's more of the same.

Michael W: I agree.

Jeff: On another note, you were talking today, Michael (White), about the performance of preferred claims. When someone consults with us and speaks of their hopes and desires for change, there is much within the therapeutic culture that can invite us to disregard these claims, to be cynical about them. What you seemed to be saying was that as therapists we could create a context for a performance of these claims and that this can make a significant difference in people's lives. Can you say a little more about this?

Michael W: I believe that to take up the opportunity to more richly describe one's quest has the effect of advancing one's quest. In this way, therapy can become a context for the performance of preferred claims about identity, about ways of being in the world – and that's our business, isn't it, to open space for people to express these claims and to contribute to establishing contexts in which these claims might be performed and acknowledged by others in ways that are authenticating of them. I understand this to be powerfully shaping of people's lives. I don't believe that it is all that helpful, to the people who consult therapists, for us to traffic in cynicism. Unfortunately young people are regularly subject to this in relation to their preferred identity claims – 'They are just saying that they want to leave all of this trouble behind because that is what they want you to think', or 'In entering this undertaking to change their ways, they are just pulling the wool over your eyes. This is just what they want you to believe'.

But we don't have to engage with this doctrine of doubt. We can respond to such identity claims in ways that are honouring of these, in ways that contribute to possibilities for people to more richly describe them, and to participate in the identification and creation forums in which these claims might be performed. We can then consult these people about what they consider to be the consequences, to their lives and relationships, of the performance of these claims, and encourage them to evaluate these consequences.

Michael H: I want to ask another basic question, if I could. I hear these days some people referring to narrative therapy as a kind of social movement, or a kind of liberation philosophy. It is being identified in some circles as politically 'left-wing'. Have you heard these sorts of things? Is it your intention for narrative therapy to be perceived in these ways?

Michael W: I have heard people reflect on narrative therapy in these ways and have some concern that such descriptions could be trivialising and diminishing of the courage expressed in, and of the very significant contributions and achievements of, various social movements. I do not know of any therapists who have risked their lives and the safety of their families, who have totally compromised their security, or who have been exiled due to their involvement in narrative therapy. And yet these experiences are often had by people who participate in social movements, and in initiatives that are informed by liberation philosophy.

And there are other reasons why the description of narrative therapy as a social movement does not fit for me. I don't know how it is that narrative therapy could be constructed as a social movement, or as a kind of liberation philosophy. Social movements, in my understanding, are broad-based and issue focussed, very often addressing wider social justice issues from a variety of political platforms. In this sense, I don't believe that there is anything about what I understand to be narrative therapy that would allow it to make any claim to be a social movement or a liberation philosophy.

As well, the liberation philosophies principally focus on the forces of oppression and repression. And, as an outcome of their association with liberal humanism, these movements usually incorporate a strong vision or narrative about how things could otherwise be in the world. Contrast this with the agenda that is explicit in narrative therapy. This is to engage in some local inquiry into what is happening, into how things are becoming other than what they were, or into the potential for things to become other than what they are. It is to engage in the rich description of the knowledges and skills of living expressed in this, and in an exploration of the possibilities, limitations and possible dangers associated with how things are and with how they are becoming other than what they were. Although I believe that this emphasis provides for a socially and politically sensitive practice, I want to reiterate that I don't believe that there is anything about these practices that could constitute narrative therapy as a social movement.

Michael H: It seems to me, if I am following you, that one distinction comes back to the ways in which narrative practices seek to provide a context for people to identify their own preferences for life and to evaluate the effects of these preferences. The people consulting therapists are making choices as to the directions in which they go rather than following an agenda or direction set by the therapist.

Michael W: I think that is part of it. It is like saying: 'Well, everything is not exactly what it seems to be', or 'Things don't have to be the way they've been' or 'There are these settled certainties that really are not all that settled'.

Michael H: I have one further question. Karl Tomm, in discussing your paper 'Deconstruction and Therapy', wrote:

> *What I would like to see more of in Michael's workshop presentations and in his written work is a readiness to openly and explicitly apply his critique of knowledge and power during his teaching. This desire arises from my interest in the second- order perspective of observing systems. Perhaps it is unreasonable of me to expect this from him in that such a critique could undermine the effectiveness of his protest against those theories and practices that he considers pathologizing. On the other hand, I often wonder whether the receptiveness of other professionals could be enhanced if he became more open and self-reflective in this respect. I must add, however, that in his clinical work Michael is very attentive to and critical of his own power. He has always carefully monitored the effects of his influence on clients and recently even began inviting clients to interview him about his questions. In doing so, he*

> invites them to become more aware of the influence he is having upon them. Nevertheless, this attention to his own power during therapy has not yet become an integral part of his workshop teaching, nor has a critique of his own power as a major contributor in the field become a part of his major presentations. Perhaps these are developments we shall see in the future. (1993)

How would you respond to Karl's concern?

Michael W: I always appreciate Karl Tomm's attention to the power relations of therapy. He is a good friend who is always offering challenges and invitations to take up questions about different issues. His voice on this issue has been very important, particularly in a field where there hasn't been anywhere near enough effort put in to addressing these questions. And I don't believe that such a critique in anyway undermines my refusal of the pathologising discourses. In fact, any reflections on the power relations in this field can only support such a critique. I agree that it would be helpful for all presenters who are in an influential position to address this influence through critique, in a way that could contribute to an exploration of the power relation that is associated with this influence, whether this be across the therapist/service seeker interface or the presenter/workshop participant interface – an exploration partly shaped by questions like: 'What are possibilities that are associated with this power relation?', 'What are its limitations', 'And what are the dangers of this power relation?'. I have been working on different approaches to this critique in relation to my own consultations and presentations, and have been encouraged in this by Karl Tomm's reflections on these consultations and presentations. Rather than contributing to an 'anything goes' sentiment, poststructuralist inquiry contributes to a 'nothing goes' sentiment – nothing goes without question, including all of the narrative practices referred to here and elsewhere, and our participation in the power relations that Karl Tomm is drawing attention to.

Michael H: Do you ever feel as if you are pathologising the pathologisers? That you're putting down the psychiatrists who diagnose others as having 'ADHD' or 'Borderline Personality Disorder'.

Michael W: To pathologise anyone requires an engagement with the discourses of psychopathology and with very distinct, very well known, structuralist practices. I do my best not to engage with either (although, this does not mean that I am not engaged in the reproduction of power relations). I have not 'put-down' psychiatrists, psychologists, social workers, counsellors or professional schools or the particular affiliations of any professional discipline. And I have not taken a position for or against labels. Rather, I have been interested to understand what these labels mean to people, what they make possible, who they serve best and least, and to explore the real and potential limitations and dangers of these labels. But I have always questioned the pathologising discourses that are so routinely dishonouring of people's lives, and that marginalise and disqualify the knowledges and skills that people bring with them into the therapeutic arena, knowledges and skills that have been generated in the history of their lives and their relationships with others. And I have continued to challenge the taken-for-granted practices of immodesty of the culture of psychotherapy.

Jeff: I think it's important to think through how we challenge pathologising practices. I know that once I did not take such care in this, but now I'm very careful to be respectful in this process.

Michael W: Let me just add, that in the questioning and challenging of pathologising practices, I have not been at all interested in playing any part in the construction of new norms around which therapists might be encouraged or required to measure and evaluate themselves. To continue to raise these questions and to take up this challenge is not specifying of other therapists' practices. There is a world of options for engaging with people seeking consultation that don't reproduce the discourses of psychopathology.

Michael H: That seems a good note to finish up on! Thank you, Michael and Jeff. I have really appreciated having the opportunity to join with you in this discussion.

References

Bachelard, G. 1969: *The Poetics of Space*. Boston: Beacon Press.

Cowley, G. & Springen, K. 1995, April 17: 'Rewriting life stories.' *Newsweek*, pp.70-74.

Geertz, C. 1986: 'Making experiences, authoring selves.' In V. Turner & E. Bruner (eds), *The Anthropology of Experience*. Chicago: University of Illinois Press.

Hare-Mustin, R. 1992: 'Cries and whispers: The psychotherapy of Anne Sexton.' *Psychotherapy*, 29:406-409.

Hare-Mustin, R. 1994: 'Discourse in the mirrored room: A postmodern analysis of therapy.' *Family Process*, 33:19-35.

Hoffman. L. 1993: *Exchanging Voices: A collaborative approach to family therapy*. London: Karnac Books.

Hoyt, M.F. (ed) 1994: *Constructive Therapies*. New York: Guilford Press.

Hoyt, M.F. (ed) 1996: *Constructive Therapies, Volume 2*. New York: Guilford Press.

Hoyt, M.F. (ed) 1998: *The Handbook of Constructive Therapies*. San Francisco: Jossey-Bass.

Hoyt, M.F. 2000: *Some Stories are Better than Others: Doing what works in brief therapy and managed care*. Philadelphia: Brunner/Mazel.

Minuchin, S. 1992: 'The restoried history of family therapy.' In J.K. Zeig (ed), *The Evolution of Psychotherapy: The second conference* (pp. 3-12). New York: Brunner/Mazel.

Simon, R. 1996: 'It's more complicated than that: An interview with Salvador Minuchin.' *Family Therapy Networker*, 20(6):50-56.

Tomm, K. 1993: 'The courage to protest: A commentary on Michael White's work.' In S. Gilligan & R. Price (eds), *Therapeutic Conversations* (pp. 62-80). New York: Norton.

White, M. 1995: *Re-Authoring Lives: Interviews and essays*. Adelaide: Dulwich Centre Publications.

White, M., Hoyt, M.F. & Combs, G. 1996: 'On ethics and the spiritualities of the surface: A conversation with Michael White.' In M.F. Hoyt (ed), *Constructive Therapies, Volume 2* (pp. 33-59). New York: Guilford Press.

Zimmerman, J. & Dickerson, V.C. 1996: *If Problems Talked: Narrative therapy in action*. New York: Guilford Press.

7.

Then and now ...*

Interviewer: Jill Freedman**

Jill: I'm going to ask you some very broad questions, Michael, and we'll only have room to print partial answers. Keeping that in mind, could you describe where you were twenty-five years ago, theoretically and clinically, and where you are now? There might be some strand you'd be interested in that you could follow over twenty-five years.

Michael: Oh, I think there are definitely strands that can be traced through those twenty-five years. Twenty-five years ago I was working in a large state psychiatric hospital that provided very few services for people. When I arrived there, I quickly reached the conclusion that the people who were in this hospital were mostly people in circumstances of disadvantage in the community – people with very few resources available to them. I wanted to understand what was happening for the families of people who had been given various diagnoses, including schizophrenia. I wanted to understand what was happening for these families in terms of their contexts of life. It wasn't that I couldn't

---

* This interview was first published in *AFTA Newsletter* (volume #74, Winter Issue, 1998/89, pp.43-47).
** Jill Freedman is the Co-director of the Evanston Family Therapy Centre, and (with Gene Combs) is co-author of *Symbol, Story and Ceremony* (1990) and *Narrative Therapy: The Social Construction of Preferred Realities* (1996).

entertain medical or physiological explanations for some of the experiences that these people were going through, but it became clear to me the circumstances of the lives of the greater majority of these people were pretty stressful and that this was a significant factor contributing to their various predicaments.

Relatives were not on the map at all in terms of services for people at this hospital, so I started to meet with families. Soon the demand for this service was such that I decided to meet with groups of families. Before long, these meetings were taking place in the local community, not in the hospital. Although in the first place the focus of these meeting was directed on the concerns of the people in these groups, in a short while it would shift to community action – to people getting organised to support others in their communities who were experiencing hard times.

Jill: How did these family groups start meeting in the community?

Michael: It seemed like a logical process. The people in the family group meetings were addressing the circumstances of their lives, and these were circumstances that predominated in the communities in which they lived. It made sense, then, to meet in these communities. There were lots of wonderful outcomes of those meeting for the families of these groups, but also for other people who had fallen on hard times.

Jill: Can you talk about one of those outcomes?

Michael: There was a state housing authority community that had few services and virtually no amenities. The local primary school was alongside a busy highway that had no school crossing. It was not safe for the children, but who was going to listen to this communities complaints about this? So the families of this group, almost entirely headed by sole parent mothers, moved on this. They blocked the highway on a Friday evening of a long weekend when everyone was pouring out of the city. They blocked the highway with their babies and prams, their children and tricycles, their pets, and even their household furniture! It was an extraordinary event.

Jill: Wow!

Michael: And it was successful. They got a school crossing. And they engaged in many other actions as well. It was really inspiring to me to see these people who were otherwise disadvantaged building solidarity and joining with each other, not just to care for their own community, but to insist that their community was cared for by local authorities.

Back then I had great difficulty in appreciating the distinctions that were so often made between counselling/therapy, community work, and social action. I have the very same difficulty today.

Jill: Do you have any thoughts about how it was that issues of social disadvantage stood out for you rather than psychiatric diagnoses in the context of a psychiatric hospital?

Michael: I think that growing up in a working-class community contributed something to this. I believe that in such communities there is often less of a contrast between private and public lives. In middle- and upper middle-class contexts, the problems and struggles of people's lives can be relatively easily hidden from view. In these contexts there are resources available to apply to this end. For example, if a man physically abuses his woman partner, she can withdraw from circulation until the signs of this abuse are healed. Or other resources can be taken up in contributing to a successful cover-up. But in the community that I grew up in, such resources were not available – who could retreat in this way when resources were spread thin, and when day-to-day living depended so much upon people pressing ahead with their tasks, in the factories or elsewhere. In these circumstances, when the private and the public are drawn so close, the contexts of people's 'problems' were highly visible – these problems invariably made sense to anybody who cared to look.[1]

In my social work training, which I began in 1967, I became very interested in the work of a number of figures who contributed to my thinking about context, including Erving Goffman. And his work I still respect greatly. Also, there was something about the spirit of the times that helped me to develop and maintain a consciousness of local politics. It was the era of the Vietnam war and of the student protest movement.

Jill: So that was very natural to include in your work?

Michael: Yeah, at the time, yeah.

Jill: Okay. And that would be a strand that's been there throughout these last twenty-five years?

Michael: Well, I got separated from it in the middle part of the seventies when I was caught up in ideas about legitimate practice and in work contexts in which there was a strong expectation, in fact a requirement, that one would relate one's work to a known 'model'. So I side-stepped into explorations of some of the 'schools' of family therapy. I engaged with these schools through the mid to late seventies, and then disengaged from them and again picked up the strand or the thread that we have been talking about. I still regret this separation. However, I am not thinking that this side-step was fruitless. For one thing, it introduced me to contributions of some of the figures in the field who were able to think outside of what was routinely thought at the time.

Jill: Although you have developed your own ways of working, were some of the ideas of the established models of family therapy important in that?

Michael: If we are talking about ideas, there are some continuities that can be traced, but I think that the discontinuities are more significant. I don't have the idea that the history of family therapy is one of evolution in which certain ideas or theoretical developments provide the foundation for the next and so on. There are too many contradictions to this narrative of progression.

But I do strongly value my engagement with family therapy. It is clear to me that in this field it has been possible, to an extent, for people to think outside of what was otherwise being thought at the time. In fact, I believe this has been encouraged. Perhaps this could be identified as a tradition, or as a spirit of adventure and exploration. So, for me, standing on the inside of what I think and do, what I appreciate most strongly is the contribution of those figures that have shaped such a fertile context – to the shaping of a context that is fertile in the sense that it accommodates a whole range of ideas that are often discontinuous, at times contradictory, and frequently novel. This is a context in which ideas are not spontaneously rejected because they don't fit with what has been already established. I believe this to be something that we can celebrate.

When I think about the figures that have contributed to this tradition, so many come to mind: Jay Haley, Virginia Satir, Salvador Minuchin, Mara Selvini Palazzoli, Luigi Boscolo, Gianfranco Cecchin, Peggy Papp, Olga Silverstein, Lyn Hoffman, Paul Watzlawick and John Weakland, to name just a few. And most of these people continue to contribute to this tradition, and to the further development of ideas and practices. At these times when I am naming names I always feel disconcerted – I find myself thinking of all the other names that should also be in here.

Jill: Yeah. I think the feminist critique, which has also found a home in family therapy, has been really important in narrative work as well, particularly in exposing power relations.

Michael: Yeah. I agree.

Jill: Okay, so what do you think is the most important change or shift you have made?

Michael: I think it was a shift back ... well, it wasn't that I ceased to acknowledge power relations in a general sense, but a shift to take that acknowledgement back into my work more.
 At times I hear it said that my work brings politics or issues of power into therapy. I've received invitations to join panels at conferences to debate whether it's the therapist's place to bring politics into therapy – that is, politics with a lower case 'p': the politics of gender, of race, of culture, of heterosexual dominance, or of disadvantage, or whatever. Sometimes I am invited to these debates because there is some account of me at large that I am political in the sense of being correct or in terms of 'setting others straight', which is not what it is about for me at all. I am interested in the opportunities that are available to join with people in questioning what they routinely think and do with each other.
 I always decline to enter debates according to these terms. It seems an absurd idea to me to propose that the therapeutic context is one where culture is absent, that in this context people are not reproducing the power relations of local culture in some way, or that the therapist is exempt from contributing to

the reproduction of these power relations. It is not a matter of whether the therapist bring politics into therapy. It is a matter of whether they are prepared to acknowledge the power relations of local culture that are being reproduced in the therapeutic context.

I have been more prepared to enter conversations that address the questions: Is it the therapist's role to play a part in obscuring the power relations of culture? Is it the therapist's role to render invisible the context of people's experiences of life? Is it the therapist's role to be complicit in the reproduction of the power relations of local culture? What is the outcome of the therapist's claims to an innocent bystander status? What are the politics of such a role and such a claim?

Jill: Me too.

Michael: I don't know if that is the major shift. It is not a shift in the sense that it is something entirely new. It's more to do with reclaiming some things that I got separated from that I regret having been separated from.

Jill: I think another shift, at least in my experience of your work, is really thinking about one's work in communities rather than in isolation.

Michael: I would see that as a trend because increasingly over the years I've been engaging with a sense of community in my work with people. I might start off with two or three people in my room and often this number grows as the therapy proceeds, sometimes through the presence of relatives, friends, acquaintances or others who are invited to join according to special purposes.

Recently I was meeting with a young man, Simon, who was making yet another effort to address a pervasive depression that had 'dogged' his late adolescence and adult years. He shared with me his understanding of the history of this depression – his mother had suicided when he was six years of age. Simon told me that he had done a lot of work on this issue, addressing his sense of guilt over this. He had also learned, in the context of therapy, that his depression was in part an expression of internalised anger that was an outcome of rage at his mother's 'betrayal' of him. It was clear that these understandings hadn't been all that helpful to Simon. I asked Simon to tell me about the circumstances of his mother's life. He knew that life had been a struggle for her – she had grown up in difficult and discouraging circumstances, had been abandoned by Simon's father, and then by the father of his two siblings.

Not long into our conversation, we were talking about some of the dreams that Simon had once had for his life. Over the next twenty or thirty minutes I asked questions that encouraged Simon to trace the history of these dreams. Suddenly he was telling me a couple of stories about his relationship with his mother. These were very slim but touching stories, and although Simon was tearful through the telling of these, this appeared to be enlivening of him.

The story of Simon's mother reminded me of a woman, Jan, who had consulted me about three months earlier – she had made a significant attempt to kill herself but had been saved by the quick thinking of a neighbour. Jan had three children whom she loved dearly, but just couldn't see a way out of the dire straights that she had been in and thought that her children would be better off in the hands of her relatives. Jan stepped into some therapeutic conversations and quickly reclaimed her life and her place with her children, and broke from isolation. Without contravening the principle of confidentiality, I wondered whether Simon would be interested in meeting with me and a woman who might help us to speculate further on the circumstances of his mothers life and her suicide. He decided to give it a go, and when I contacted Jan about the idea she was enthusiastic to play a part. We had three rather extraordinary meetings together (the third was also attended by Jan's children and by Simon's siblings), the outcome of which Simon began to remember many more stories about his mothers care for and love of him. This proved to be an antidote to his depression. By the way, these conversations also had very beneficial effects in Jan's life.

Jill: I like that story very much, but I guess we should go on. So, what are the most difficult situations you contend with and where do you go for help with challenging cases?

Michael: The first thing I'm likely to do is consult the people who are consulting me about the difficulties in the work that we share. That doesn't mean that I don't value what other professional people have to contribute to addressing these difficulties. I'm in conversation with them as well. But the first point of entry for me is to consult with the people who are consulting me.

Jill: You know, one of the things that I do first if I feel like I'm stuck in a difficult situation is call upon an outsider-witness group or a reflecting team.

Michael: Yeah. I'm often in contexts where I have the luxury of the presence of an outsider- witness group. Not only do the people who are consulting me get many ideas from the retellings of these groups, but I also get ideas that I consistently find very helpful. At times these ideas carry us past whatever might have been limiting of our explorations

Jill: I'm wondering about the first part of the question. Are there some situations that are most difficult situations for you?

Michael: Some of the more difficult situations have to do with working with men who are referred to me for perpetrating abuse and who are very much at one with abusive practices. At times, in the first place, there appears to be few options to engage these men in questioning these abusive ways. It can take a little time to find avenues for joining with these men in ways that assist them to get in touch with other values, other purposes, and other visions for their life and their relationships; other values, purposes and visions that are also part of their history, but that don't fit at all well with the abusive practices they've been engaging in.

Initially, it can be somewhat difficult to join with these men to help them find somewhere else to stand so that they can critique the abuse that they have reproduced, so that they can address their responsibility to develop a consciousness for the real effects of what they have done, and so that they can find ways of mending what might be mended.

Jill: Can you just talk about that difficulty a bit more?

Michael: For me sometimes the difficulty relates to how to join with these men in a different territory of their lives that speaks to caring, understanding and loving ways of being – to find thin traces of these other ways of being in their lives and to join with them in thickening these traces, so that they can begin to take a position against the abusive ways of being that they have been visiting on other people's lives. I think that can be quite a task at times.

Jill: I do too ... The next question is about how significant life events or developmental stages have had an impact on your work. Or other ways your life influences your work? And, of course, how does your work influence your life?

Michael: I'm curious about the distinction that is drawn between life and work. I'm not suggesting that there are no limits, but, although I do live out my life in different social domains, I can't possibly see how these can be anything but joined. I have experiences in my work that significantly contribute to the shaping of my life. The life that I live out in other domains is richer for the life that I live in the therapeutic domain. And my life in the therapeutic domain is richer for the experiences of living that I have in the other domains of my life. It is important for me to identify the ways in which my experience of my work shape my life more generally, and to identify how the experiences that I have in other domains of life shape my conversations with the people who consult me. It is important not just to identify this, but also to find ways of acknowledging it. Otherwise, many of the really sparkling events that are potentially shaping who I am in different domains of living remain just that – unrealised.

Jill: Would you like to speak of an event that touched your life?

Michael: Yeah. I was recently consulted by a heterosexual couple. The man, whom I will call Daniel, was very sad and said that he had felt lost for some time. But now he was more than lost. He was despairing and couldn't see any horizon to his life. Daniel's partner, Maureen, had been increasingly concerned about him and was now at her wit's end, not knowing what to do. I came to understand that this despair spoke to the fact that he had recently lost touch with some of the 'guiding hopes' that he'd held for himself as a man, and for how he could be with Maureen.

In endeavouring to help me understand how he had been introduced to these guiding hopes – his own father and paternal grandfather had been very abusive – Daniel told me a beautiful story. It was a story about how his uncle John (this uncle was one of his mother's cousins) used to visit the family home from time to time. These visits were irregular, and would always be 'out of the blue'. Uncle John seemed to know what Daniel's mother was going through. He was kind to her. Uncle John also seemed fond of Daniel as he would always bring him a present of a small treat or a toy. He would even join Daniel in playing with the toy. This was a fondness and gentleness that was quite distinct in relation to anything that Daniel had experienced from any other man.

Daniel's recounting of this story was quite emotional. In relation to this recounting, we had the opportunity to explore many things. We speculated about why it was that Uncle John had attended to Daniel in the way that he did, about what it was about Daniel that Uncle John might have appreciated, and about how Uncle John might respond to the knowledge that he had significantly contributed to the guiding hope that Daniel had treasured. In this conversation, Daniel reclaimed this guiding hope, and his despair dissipated.

Daniel hadn't seen his Uncle John, who was now a very old man who lived in a small interstate country town, for some years. Daniel decided to visit him with the intention of speaking with him about the significance of what he had introduced Daniel to – another world of being for Daniel as a man. It turned out to be a wonderful reunion, and Daniel brought back to me a message and a gift from his uncle – a bag of oranges picked from his own tree. Having travelled 600 miles in the heat of summer, the oranges weren't in great shape by the time they got to me. But I was so touched by this gift.

I'm not sure that experiences like these are so generally available to people in the usual run of life. As therapists, we are in such a privileged position. Just the other day, I was in the workshop here and there was a bowl of oranges. Someone picked up one of these oranges and began to peel it. The scent of this re-evoked the experience of being touched by Daniel's uncle. I treasure this. I am sure that this affected what went on in the workshop that morning. And, hopefully, it contributed to my being more conscious of the acts of inclusion that I experience from people in this work.

Jill: Yeah. Yeah. One of our questions is: Is this influence more or less true now than it was when you began practicing? And I guess I was wondering in line with this if there is something about the way you practice now that supports treasuring those kinds of experiences – being let into people's lives – that maybe there was something in the other ideas that wouldn't allow that to happen as much, or was it always that way for you?

Michael: I think there are today lots of ideas about boundaries and about ethics that take us away from this. What's called ethics today is all about top-down regulations, rules and guidelines that not only make us less accountable to the people who consult us, but also make it very difficult for us to relate to and to embrace many a wonderful contribution to our lives from these people. I am not saying that we can do without some rules or regulations, but I'm concerned about how rules, regulations and global principles have supplanted considerations of personal ethics. It is now even possible to do ethics courses in universities without ever engaging with personal ethics!

Jill: Speaking of the way the field is going, what contemporary work do you think will be important in the future?

Michael: I hope that there will be further developments in the field that could help us to break from the theorising of other people's lives. I hope that we will be able to take in more of the developments from other disciplines that relate to what's often called the 'interpretive turn'. The interpretive turn has to do with resisting expert-knowledge interpretations of life and has to do with bringing to the centre the meanings of the people who consult us, and the contexts in which those meanings are generated, regenerated and revisioned.

Jill: Thanks Michael, I've enjoyed our conversation.

Note

1. This doesn't mean that all was public. I have no doubt that there was some successful concealment in the community that I grew up in.

8.

On ethics and the spiritualities of the surface·

Interviewers**: Michael F. Hoyt*** & Gene Combs****

Michael H: I was very moved by the eloquence of your presentation this afternoon. I thought it was practical love. That's what came to my mind: love in practice.

Michael W: I can relate to descriptions like this, and believe that we need to be reclaiming these sorts of terms in the interpretation of what we are doing – love, passion, compassion, reverence, respect, commitment, and so on. Not because

---

* Originally published in M.F. Hoyt (ed), *Constructive Therapies, Volume 2*. New York: Guilford Press, 1996. Reproduced here with permission.

** The following conversation took place on July 16, 1994, at the Therapeutic Conversations 2 conference held in Reston, Virginia (near Washington, D.C.), where Michael White was serving as a core faculty member. An hour before the conversation, Michael White had presented a workshop on 'Consulting Our Consultants'.

*** Michael Hoyt is a California-based psychologist. He is the author of *Brief Therapy and Managed Care* (1995), and *Some Stories are Better than Others* (2000); editor of *Constructive Therapies*, Vol.1 & 2 (1994, 1996), and *The Handbook of Constructive Therapies* (1998); and the co-editor of *The First Session in Brief Therapy* (1992).

**** Gene Combs is the Co-director of the Evanston Family Therapy Centre and (with Jill Freedman) is co-author of *Symbol, Story and Ceremony* (1990) and *Narrative Therapy: The Social Construction of Preferred Realities* (1996).

love and passion are enough, but because these terms are emblematic of certain popular discourses; because they are associated with discursive fields that are constituted of alternative rules about what counts as legitimate knowledge, about who is authorised to speak of these knowledges, about how these knowledges might be expressed – including the very manner of speaking of them, about in which contexts these knowledges might be expressed, and so on. And these discursive fields are also constituted of different technologies for the expression of, or for the performance of, these knowledges – different techniques of the self, and different practices of relationship. So, what I am saying is that terms of description like love and passion are emblematic of discourses that can provide a point of entry to alternative modes of life, to specific ways of being and thinking; which will have different real effects on the shape of the therapeutic interaction, different real effects on the lives of the people who consult us, and different real effects on our lives as well.

The rise of the 'therapeutic disciplines' has been associated with extraordinary development in the discourses of science, and, of course, in the modern technologies of relationship. So notions of love and of passion haven't been considered relevant to what we might do in the name of therapy. Because we have become alienated from terms of description such as these, the popular discourses that they are emblematic of have not been all that constitutive of our work; these discourses have not had a significant effect on the shape of mainstream therapeutic practices in recent history.

Michael H: Watching you work, I had the thought that in India people put their hands together and they say *Namaste* – 'I salute the divine in you' – meaning 'What the story on the surface is, I see something holy or special'. If you're a Christian you'd say, 'It's the Christ in you' – although I'm not particularly Christian. Watching you work, I keep seeing over and over in the tapes and the discussion with the audience how you hear the positive. I just want to ask you, how you keep doing that? This has been a very congenial audience, but sometimes the patients are unpleasant, they are challenging, they've done miserable things, they've hurt people, abused people, and yet you're able to treat them with this respect, to kind of separate them from the culture that's been imposed on them. Where does that come from? How can I, how can other people, do more of that? Is there a sort of a key or clue that would help us look at people more that way?

Michael W: These are important questions. You have asked two questions. The first was about the spiritual piece, is that right?

Michael H: Yeah. What I'm getting at is not necessarily that we have to be 'spiritual' or 'religious', but it's looking at people and seeing something in them that's more than the story they're presenting, being able to see the positive underneath all this misery and stuff, seeing there's something good there.

Michael W: The notion of spirituality does interest me. In the histories of the world's cultures there have been many different notions of spirituality. I won't attempt to provide an account of these as I've not had the opportunity to study them, and I don't believe that I have even established an adequate grasp of the dominant notions of spirituality in the recent history of my own culture, or for that matter, in the history of my experience. But I am aware of the extent to which spirituality, in this western culture, has been cast in *immanent forms*, *ascendant forms*, and in *immanent/ascendant forms*.

Ascendant forms of spirituality are achieved on planes that are imagined at an altitude above everyday life. It is when people succeed in rising to these altitudes that they experience God's blessing, whomever that god might be. It is on these planes that an understanding of what would approximate a direct correspondence between God's word and one's life is attainable; it is on this plane that it becomes possible to achieve a relatively unmediated expression of God's word.

Immanent forms of spirituality are achieved not by locating oneself at some altitude above one's life, but by descending into the caverns that are imagined deep below the surface of one's life. This is a spirituality that is achieved by 'being truly and wholly who one really is', 'by being in touch with one's true nature', by being faithful to the god of self. Much of popular psychology is premised on a version of this notion of an immanent spirituality – to worship a self through being at one with one's 'nature'.

And then there are *immanent/ascendant forms* of spirituality, in which spirituality is achieved by being in touch with or having an experience of a soul or the divine that is deep within oneself and that is manifest through one's relationship with a god who is ascendant.

These and other novel contemporary notions of spirituality are of a non-material form. They propose spiritualities that are relatively intangible, that are split apart from the material world, that manifest themselves on planes that are imagined above or below the surface of life as it is lived. Although I find many of the contemporary immanent/ascendant notions of spirituality to be quite beautiful, and the notion of the soul far more aesthetically pleasing than the notion of the psyche, and although I remain interested in exploring the proposals for life or, if you like, the ethics, that are associated with these notions of spirituality, I am more interested in what might be called the material versions of spirituality. Perhaps we could call these the *spiritualities of the surface.*

The spiritualities of the surface have to do with material existence. These are the spiritualities that can be read in the shape of people's identity projects, in the steps that people take in the knowing formation of the self. This is a form of spirituality that concerns one's personal ethics, that concerns the modes of being and thought that one enters one's life into, that is reflected in the care that one takes to attain success in a style of living. This is a transformative spirituality in that it so often has to do with becoming other than the received version of who one is. This is a form of spirituality that relates not to the non-material, but to the tangible. And I believe that this is the sort of spirituality to which Foucault referred in his work on the ethics of the self (1988a, 1988b).

So, to return to your question. When I talk of spirituality I am not appealing to the divine or the holy. And I am not saluting human nature, whatever that might be, if it does exist at all. The notion of spirituality that I am relating to is one that makes it possible for me to see and to appreciate the visible in people's lives, not the invisible. It is a notion of spirituality that makes it possible for us to appreciate those events of people's lives that just might be, or might provide for, the basis for a knowing formation of the self according to certain ethics. The notion of spirituality that I am relating to is one that assists us to attend to the material options for breaking from many of the received ways of life, to attend to those events of people's lives that provide the basis for the constitution of identities that are other than those which are given. And in this sense it is a spirituality that has to do with relating to one's material options in a way that one becomes more conscious of one's own knowing.

I hope that this answer to your question is not too obscure, but this provides some account of what spirituality is about for me.

Michael H: No, your response is not obscure. I get the essence. It is about knowing self-formation.

Michael W: Yes. For me a notion of spirituality would have to be about this. It is about the exploration of the options for living one's life in ways that are other in regard to the received modes of being. It is to do with the problematising of the taken-for-granted, the questioning of the self-evident. At times it is about the refusal of certain forms of individuality, about the knowing transgression of the limits of the 'necessary' ways of being in the world; about the exploration of alternative ways of being, and of the distinct habits of thought and of life associated with these ways of being. In many ways it is about seizing upon indeterminacy, and about the re-invention of who we are. And it is about prioritising the struggle with the moral and ethical questions relating to all of this.

Gene: The thing I'm interested in is how people decide which of those possibilities to privilege, and I think that's one of the places where therapists, whether they want to or not, are given power. To become one who one has not been could go in an infinite number of directions.

Michael W: It could, I agree.

Gene: What can you say about what your experience is, what you're guided by? Which of those directions to privilege?

Michael W: In the work itself, this is achieved by consulting people about the particularities of those alternative ways of being. This is to be in ongoing consultation with people about the real effects of specific ways of being in their relationships with others and on the shape of their lives generally. I don't think the goal is to settle on some specific 'other' way of being in the world, to 'fix' one's life. This work engages people with others in ongoing revisions of their images about who they might be, and about how they might live their lives. And it engages people in an ongoing critique of notions of identity that are based on our cultures many naturalised ideas about this. In fact, this work opens options for people to divest their lives of many of these notions. And in so doing, raises options for people to explore the possibilities for disengaging from the sort of modern practices of self evaluation that have them locating their lives on the continuums of growth and development, of health and normality, of dependence and independence, and so on. These options can also constitute a refusal to engage in those modern acts of self-government that have us living out our lives under the canopy of the bell-shaped curve.

Michael H: So we offer them, 'You know, you don't have to be this way. You could continue in the path you're in, but there are alternatives. Would you like to look at those?' Is that ...

Michael W: Yes. Well I guess so, in a fairly crude way of putting it. I think it is about actually joining with people in the knowing exploration of, and the performance of, options for ways of being in life that might be available to them. It is to engage with people in a choice-making, about these options, that is based on expressions of their lived-experience and on expressions of alternative knowledges of life.

Michael H: When we use invitations or wondering or externalising or any kind of deconstructing[1], it seems to me we're still in some way highlighting certain options or suggesting, 'You may want to consider this' – putting it crudely – and that gets into the power differential. Are we in some way subtly suggesting which alternatives they might take?

Michael W: Of course we are influential, and of course there is a power differential. And it has often been claimed that because of this there can be no way of differentiating between different therapeutic practices on the basis of subjugation; that because of this fact of influence and because of this fact of power, one therapeutic practice cannot be distinguished from another; that there is a certain equity between all therapeutic practices in terms of their real effects. But this blurring of important distinctions around forms and degrees of influence within the therapeutic context is unfortunate. In fact, I believe the blurring of this distinction to be a profoundly conservative act that permits the perpetration of domination in the name of therapy, and excuses those actions that establish therapists as unquestioning accomplices of the status-quo.

It has also been said that because we are of our cultures discourses, and that we cannot think and act outside of them, that we are condemned to reproduce, in therapy, the very relations of power and experiences of self, or subjectivities, that it might be our intent to assist people to challenge. What an extraordinarily reductionist, unitary, global, and monolithic account of culture, of life, we are being encouraged to embrace by this account. What are the real effects of this sort of argument? How does it mask contestation, and undermine struggle? In what ways does it contribute to the further marginalisation of alternative knowledges of ways of being in the world, of alternative subjectivities?

In terms of practice, there is a very significant difference between, on the one hand, delivering interventions that are based on some external formal analysis of a problem, or suggesting to people that they should work on their 'independence' or 'growth' or whatever, and, on the other hand, encouraging people to attend to some events of their lives that that just might be of a more sparkling nature – events that just might happen to contradict those plots of their lives that they find so unrewarding and dead-ended – and to ask them to reflect on what these events might say about other ways of living that might suit them and that might be available to them; to join with people in the exploration of the knowledges and practices of life that might be associated with these alternative plots, to contribute to their exploration of the alternative experiences of the self that might be associated with these knowledges and practices, and to encourage them to take stock of the proposals for action that might be associated with all of this. There is an important distinction to be drawn in regard to these two classes of response.

Aside from such distinctions, we can't pretend that we are not somehow contributing to the process. We can't pretend that we are not influential in the therapeutic interaction. There is no neutral position in which therapists can stand. I can embrace this fact by joining with people to address all of those things that they find traumatising and limiting of their lives. I can respond to what people say about their experiences of subjugation, of discrimination, of marginalisation, of exploitation, of abuse, of domination, of torture, of cruelty and so on. I can join them in action to challenge the power relations and the structures of power that support all of this. And, because the impossibility of neutrality means that I cannot avoid being 'for' something, I take the responsibility to distrust what I am for – that is, my ways of life and my ways of thought – and I can do this in many ways. For example, I can distrust what I am for with regard to the appropriateness of this to the lives of others. I can distrust what I am for in the sense that what I am for has the potential to reproduce the very things that I oppose in my relations with others. I can distrust what I am for to the extent to what I am for has a distinct location in the worlds of gender, class, race, culture, sexual preference, etc. And so on.

I can take responsibility in establishing the sort of structures that contribute to the performance of this distrust. As well, I can find ways of privileging questions in therapy that reflect this distrust over ways of asking questions that would propose my favoured ways of living. I can make it my responsibility to deconstruct my notions of life, to situate these in structures of privilege, in regard to which I can engage in some actions to dismantle.

Michael H: Let me read you a quotation, if I may:

> *There is a power differential in the therapy context and it is one that cannot be erased regardless of how committed we are to egalitarian practices. Although there are many steps that we can take to render the therapeutic interaction more egalitarian, if we believe that we can arrive at some point in which we can interact with those people who seek our help in a way that is totally outside of any power relation, then we're treading on dangerous ground.* (White, 1994, p. 76)

In addition to reflecting on and asking them to reflect on, how else can we stay aware of the ethics of our influence?

Michael W: I think through a significant confrontation with this fact – that there is a power imbalance. When I propose this confrontation, I am not suggesting that this fact be celebrated, and I am not suggesting that the acknowledgement of this fact as a justification for the use of power by the therapist. And in proposing this confrontation, I am not suggesting that distinctions can't be made in regard to different therapeutic interactions on the basis of the exercise of power and on the basis of subjugation. Instead, I am proposing a confrontation that opens possibilities for us to take steps to expose and to mitigate the toxic effects of this imbalance. I am proposing a confrontation that encourages us to explore the options that might be available to us to challenge the interactional practices and to dismantle the structures that support this power relation.

For example, we can set up the sort of 'bottom-up' accountability structures that I have discussed elsewhere (see White, 1994). We can talk with the people who consult us about the dangers and the possible limitations of that power imbalance, and we can engage them in the interpretation of our conduct with regard to this. But, I have also made the point that it would be dangerous for us to believe that it is possible to establish a therapeutic context that is free of this power relation. This would be dangerous for many reasons. It would make it possible for us to avoid the responsibility of monitoring the real effects of our interactions with people who seek our help. It would make it possible for us to deny the moral and ethical responsibilities that we have to people who seek our help, and that they don't have to us. It would make it possible for us to avoid persisting in the exploration of options for the further dismantling of the structures and the relational practices that constitute this power imbalance.

Michael H: It is through accountability structures that this can be achieved?

Michael W: Well, this is part of accountability. Doing whatever we can to render transparent some of the possible limitations and dangers of that power imbalance, and setting up structures that encourage people to monitor this. In this way we are able to more squarely face the moral and ethical responsibilities that we have in this work. And I would again emphasise that it would be perilous to attempt obscure, to ourselves, the fact of this power imbalance. This would only make it possible for us to neglect the moral and ethical responsibilities that we have to the people who consult us.

Michael H: At the beginning of the conference we were asked how would we know by the end if we 'got it'. I've come during the conference more and more to think of therapy as empowerment through conversation. I just want to ask you to reflect on that. How are you defining therapy these days? Or what's an alternative word?

Michael W: First, I'd like to address your initial comment. This idea of being able to predict where we might be at the end of a process if all goes well is, I believe, a sad idea. It is my view that this is an idea that is informed by the dominant ethic of control of contemporary culture, although I do know that many would debate this point. I figure that conferences probably wouldn't be worth going to if we knew, in advance, where we would be at the end of them. There is a certain pleasure or joy available to us in the knowledge that we can't know where we'll be at the end, in the sense that we can't know beforehand what we will be thinking at the end, in the idea that we can't know what new possibilities for action in the world might be available to us at that time. It seems to me that to engage in prediction about where we might be at the end of a process if all goes well is to obscure, and to close down, options for being somewhere else. And why obscure the options for being somewhere else?

Michael H: It could take away surprise and discovery, couldn't it?

Michael W: If I planned to go to a conference, and if I knew beforehand what I would be thinking at the end, then I wouldn't go (laughter). It is like that with this work. If I knew where we would be at the end of the session, I don't think I would do this work. And this is also true for the sort of reflecting teamwork[2] that is structured according to the narrative metaphor. If reflecting team members got together and prepared their reflections ahead of their reflections – if their reflection was in fact a performance of previously articulated reflections – then it is more likely that team members will be where they predicted they would be at the end of these reflections, and the more likely it will be that everyone will become quite bored and possibly even comatose – and I have witnessed this sort of outcome. On interviewing therapists about their experience of working in this fashion, I find that it is invariably constitutive of their working lives and relationships in ways that are experienced as undesirable.

However, if team members don't undertake these preparations, if they don't know what they will be thinking about and talking about by the time that they arrive at the end of their reflections, and if the teamwork is structured in a way that facilitates this sort of interaction, then it is more likely that their work together will contribute to the shaping of their own lives and relationships in preferred ways.

Michael H: In Zen they would say you need to keep a 'beginner's mind' (Suzuki, 1970). A fresh look, not having things preconceived.

Michael W: So that's my response to the first part of your question. I think we will experience a better outcome from conferences if they contribute to some steps towards building some foundation for some other possibilities that we might not have predicted beforehand. The second part of your question had to do with how I would define therapy. Well, I define it in different ways on different days.

Michael H: What's today's date?

Gene: The sixteenth.

Michael H: At this point in time, at this moment.

Michael W: At this very moment, just for today, I think it has to do with joining with people around issues that are particularly relevant and pressing to them. It has to do with bringing whatever skills we have available to assist people in their quest to challenge or to break from whatever it is that is that they find pressing. It is our part to work with people to assist them to identify the extent to which they are knowledged in this quest. And, it is to join with people in the exploration of how their knowledges might be expressed in addressing the predicaments that they find themselves in.

In this work, people experience being knowledged, but this is not the starting point. Experiencing this is the outcome of a process that is at once characterised by 'resurrection' and 'generation'. As therapists we play a significant role in setting up the context for this. We assist people to gain access to some of these alternative knowledges of their lives by contributing to the elevation the sub-stories or sub-plots of their lives, by contributing to the resurrection of some of the knowledges of life that are associated with historical performances of these sub-plots. And we join with people in the generation of knowledges of life through the exploration of the ways of being and thinking that are associated with these sub-plots. I have shared my proposals for this process at some length in a number of publications, and will not reiterate them here. Perhaps it would be sufficient to say here that the sub-plots of people's lives provide a route to the exploration of alternative knowledges of life.

It is our part to assist in the identification of possibilities for action that are informed by these other knowledges of life. It is also our part to encourage people to evaluate the desirability of these other ways of being and thinking, through an investigation of the particularities of the proposals for action that are informed by them, through the exploration of the particularities of a life as it is lived through and constituted by these alternative knowledges.

I don't know if this answer to your question is a particularly good or appropriate answer. And if its not a good answer, its my answer for today at least. Perhaps if we do this interview again tomorrow, I just might be able to answer your question differently at that time. This is my hope.

Gene: I guess I just want to make sure I was tracking what you were saying. So, as a therapist, you're curious about and listening for what are at the moment lesser plots, subplots, counterplots, whatever, and kind of sorting through those and exploring some of those with the person and asking them which of those might be interesting to them or useful to them?

Michael W: Yes, I guess so. People are explicitly consulted about these sub-plots of their life. If the therapist's position on these sub-plots is privileged – if the therapist's position is primary – then imposition will be the outcome, and collaboration will be not be achieved. To avoid this imposition, and to establish collaboration, before proceeding we need to know how people judge those developments that might provide a gateway to the identification and exploration of these sub-plots – do they see them as positive or negative developments, or both positive and negative, or neither positive nor negative. And we need to engage people in the naming of these sub-plots of their lives. Apart from this, it is also important that we have some understanding of why it is that people so judge these developments and these sub-plots of their lives. How do these developments fit with their preferred accounts of their purposes and values and so on?

But this is not the whole story. It is never just a matter of determining what developments might be interesting or useful to people. This is not predominantly a cognitive thing. In this work, these sub-plots of people's lives are actually experienced by those who consult us. In the course of the work itself, people live these subplots. Or, if you like, people's lives are embraced by these sub-plots. These sub-plots are not stories about life; they are not maps of the territory of life; they are not reflections of life as it is lived. These sub-plots are structures of life, and in fact become more constitutive of life.

And one further point about what is at work here. There is much that remains to be said about the language of this work, about how it evokes the images of people's lives that it does. Many of the questions that we ask about the developments of people's lives are powerfully evocative of other images of who these people might be, and other versions of their identities. These images reach back into the history of people's lived experience, privileging certain memories, and facilitate the interpretation of many previously neglected aspects of experience. So the language of the work, of the very questions that we ask, is evocative of images which trigger the reliving of experience, and this contributes very significantly to the generation of alternative story lines.

Gene: So the expertise you bring ...

Michael H: Well, Michael made a very good distinction, I thought, in the last presentation between expert knowledge, meaning 'I am the expert here', versus an expert's skills, as I took it, meaning knowing how to ask questions in a way that will let the client experience their local expertise, their local knowledge. I think that is very different from the dominant voice.

Gene: So the knowledge you bring is knowledge about how to evoke in an experiential way these alternative images.

Michael W: Yes. I have often been misrepresented on this point. I have never denied the knowledgeableness of the therapist. And I have never denied the fact of therapist skilfulness. I have, however, challenged the privileging of the therapist's knowledgeableness above the knowledgeableness of people who consult therapists. And I have critiqued the 'expert knowledges'. I have critiqued expert knowledge claims, including those that make possible the imposition of global and unitary accounts of life and the development of formal systems of analysis. I have critiqued the power relations by which these expert knowledges are installed, including those that are essential to the normalising judgement of the subject, that are so effective in the government of people's lives. Throughout this critique, I have supported what is generally referred to as, after Clifford Geertz (1983), the 'interpretive turn'.

Michael H: I had the idea that looking for the sparkling 'moments', looking for the 'unique outcomes', looking for the 'exceptions', in a way what we're trying to do is help the person build a past to support a better future, create some kind of structure under them, 'thickening', I think you were using as a phrase, kind of fleshing it out or filling it in. Do I have that idea right?

Michael W: I'm really interested in the conditions under which people might 'take a leaf out of their alternative books', rather than defining a goal and determining what steps might be necessary to reach that goal. When people get to the point of experiencing the unfolding of preferred developments in the recent history of their lives, they have some sense of where their next step might be placed. Such steps are informed by a developing appreciation of a preferred story line.

Michael H: We're making it up as we go along?

Michael W: Yes, to an extent, yes. I say 'to an extent', because, although their might be certain circumstances under which we might witness what we assume to be clear breaks from the 'known', it is rather difficult to think outside of what we specifically know, and, more generally, rather impossible to think outside of knowledge systems.

In regard to the knowing formation of our lives, it seems that we are, to an extent, dependent upon developing an account of how some of our recent steps fit together with classes of steps that can be read as unfolding in sequences through time according to some theme or perhaps plot. Even upon stepping into unfamiliar territories of identity, coherence appears to be a guiding criterion. And because of this, so is culture and its knowledges of ways of being and thinking in the world.

Michael H: Although sometimes as an alternative to the idea of evolution being a continuous process, I think we're getting now into the idea of evolution not being continuous but being discontinuous, punctuated evolution.³ Stephen Jay Gould (1980) and William Alvarez talk about how things are steady state, and something extraordinary comes along, like meteorites strike the earth stirring up dust which kills the plant-eating dinosaurs, then that wipes out the meat eaters, and that opens the niche for mammals. There can be a sudden shift or something can be discontinuous. I relate this to page six of *Narrative Means to Therapeutic Ends* (White & Epston, 1990), in that table where you talk about 'before-and-after', 'betwixt-and-between', the whole 'rites of passage' idea.⁴ Sometimes we see people who feel prisoners of the path they have been on it so long, and how can they leap off it? So, there's these submerged paths, I take from what you're saying, that remind them of other routes.

Michael W: Yes, there are these sudden shifts, these apparent discontinuities. And at these junctures we can feel quite lost. Perhaps it is useful to think of this experience as a liminal or betwixt-and-between phase, one that is understandably confusing and disorienting. There is always a distance between the point of separation and the point of reincorporation. But the question remains: Is it possible to break with something without stepping into other ways of being and thinking that are not in some way continuous with something else? Is it possible to step apart from familiar modes of life and of thought and to step into some cultural vacuum, one that is free of contexts of intelligibility? Historical reflection suggests that there are very few sites of radical discontinuity. But there are always margins of possibility.

Michael H: I see what you are saying. We take something as well as separate from something.

Michael W: Yes. We step into other modes of life and of thought that go before us. But I believe that there are opportunities for us to contribute to the 'drift' of these modes of life and of thought, as we live them, through processes that relate to the negotiation of the different subjectivities or experiences of the self that are associated with these, through interpretation, and through the management of indeterminacy.

Perhaps we could say that within continuity there is discontinuity. And this consideration takes us back to the discussion that preceded these comments.

I have a problem with the idea of converting metaphors that come from the non-living world, and from biology for that matter, into the realm of human life, which is the realm of practice and of meaning, and a realm of achievement. I don't believe that this is ever a realm of how things just happen to be. For example, the achievement aspects of this realm can be witnessed in the work that people put into attributing meaning to a whole range of experiences, and the extent to which many of their actions are prefigured on this.

Michael H: Rather than mechanising or animalising or taking us to where we're not.

Michael W: Exactly. And I can't think of one metaphor from the non-living world that I think is appropriate to human life and human organisation, to people who live in culture, who live in language, who participate in making meanings that are constitutive of their lives together. But I don't know if this is relevant to this interview or not.

Michael H: It is now. (Laughter)

Michael W: Can I just come back to a point that was made earlier? Gene, around the time that we were talking about the image, you asked me about the nature of this work. What was this question again?

Gene: I was trying to imagine how it is that you conceptualise what it is that you do, what it is that you bring to the therapy situation, and I was also just trying to experience as much as I could for myself what it would be like to be you being a therapist. What am I thinking I should do next? To what am I listening?

Michael H: What is going on in Michael's head when he is working?

Gene: Yeah.

Michael W: 'To what am I listening?' is a good question. And I would say that my listening is informed by some of my preferred metaphors for this work. I particularly relate to poetics. I could read you a piece on poetics by David Malouf, because it fits so well with my conception of this work, and because he says it so much better than I could.

Michael H: Please.

Michael W: (searches in his bag and pulls out a type-written page) This is a piece from a book called *The Great World* (Malouf, 1991). This book is substantially about men's experience of Australian men's culture. In it David Malouf talks about how poetry speaks:

> *How it spoke up, not always in the plainest terms, since that wasn't always possible, but in precise ones just the same, for what is deeply felt and might otherwise go unrecorded: all of those unique and repeatable events, the little sacraments of daily existence, movements of the heart and invitations of the close but inexpressible grandeur and terror of things, that is our other history, the one that goes on, in a quiet way, under the noise and chatter of events and is the major part of what happens every day in the life of the planet, and has been from the very beginning. To find words for that; to make glow with significance what is usually unseen, and unspoken to: that, when it occurs, is what binds us all, since it speaks immediately out of the centre of each one of us; giving shape to what we too have experienced and did not till then have words for, though as soon as they are spoken we know them as our own.*

I so relate to this invocation of the 'little sacraments of daily existence'. The word *sacrament* invokes mystery. And it evokes a sense of the sacred significance of the little events of people's lives; those little events that lie in the shadows of the dominant plots of people's lives, those little events that are so often neglected, but that might come to be regarded with reverence, and at times with awe. These little sacraments are those events that have everything to do with the maintenance of a life, with the continuity of a life, often in the face of circumstances that would otherwise deny this.

These little sacraments of people's lives can be read for what they might tell us all about existence, about the particularities of how we exist. I don't believe that there is such a thing as 'mere existence'. Existing is something that we all do, and have obviously been doing now for many, many years. But it has, in so many ways, had such bad press in recent decades. Why is this the case?

Why is it becoming so hard for us to read and to appreciate the little sacraments of daily life? Perhaps this is because these sacraments are on the other side of our culture's ethic of control. Perhaps it is because these little sacraments of daily life don't relate all that well to the accepted goals for life in this culture – like demonstrating 'control over one's life'. And perhaps it is because they don't fit with contemporary definitions of the sort of actions that count as responsible actions. I believe that through the metaphor of poetics it becomes possible for us to challenge the marginalising of existence, and to all play some part in the honouring of the those facts that Malouf refers to as the 'little sacraments of daily existence'.[5]

Gene: When you say 'the little sacraments of daily existence' and you talk about finding the words, I find myself thinking about the close of Ken Gergen's (1994) talk this morning. I don't know that it in any way relates to this. He was talking about inchoate experience, that experience that's not yet quite language and yet that is just before. Does that in any way relate to what you're talking about, sort of the next step of making that, sitting with somebody and then bringing that in a language, bringing that into society?

Michael W: What Malouf is saying about the little facts of daily life fits, I believe, with the notion of the 'spiritualities of the surface' that we have been discussing. But I don't know whether or not what I am saying here has any relation to what Ken Gergen was saying. But it might, and I would like to understand more about what he is proposing before responding to your question.

Michael H: It's the 'poetics of experience' as well as the 'politics of experience'.

Michael W: Yes, it is that as well.

Michael H: I heard Robert Bly, the poet, read a long beautiful evocative poem, and someone stood up in an audience and said, 'Robert, what did it mean?' Bly said, 'If I knew what it meant I would have written an essay, not a poem!' (laughter) I thought what Gergen was getting at was the same that special moment, the sacrament, I think some people call it the spirit of life, when it's *happening* rather than just ... I'll have to ask him.

Michael W: It will be interesting to hear what he says.[6]

Michael H: I once asked Ronnie Laing what he thought of transference. I said, 'What's your definition of it or what do you think of it?' He said, 'Oh, it's post-hypnotic suggestion with amnesia'. (Laughter) Post-hypnotic suggestion with amnesia, which I relate to the whole idea of *mystification* (Laing, 1967), that we've been sort of programmed or given this suggestion of how to take things, and we don't even remember that we are given it, so we're kind of locked in. I just wanted to ask if that, from a very different frame, is a way of talking about deconstructing? Does deconstructing get one to the consciousness where you recognise you've been, to use a modern word, programmed?

Michael W: Yes. This is a take on the practices of deconstruction that I can relate to. And I would like here to pick up Laing's contribution to the deconstruction of what we are talking about when we are talking about the phenomenon of transference. The notion of 'post-hypnotic suggestion with amnesia' does bring forth the history of the interactional politics that are generative of this phenomenon, and this encourages us to think of the 'technologies of transference' as technologies of power. And, needless to say, since transference is a phenomenon that is invariably psychologised, to bring forth the technologies of transference does serve to deconstruct this.

But these technologies of transference are not just the historical conditions for the constitution of the transference phenomenon. Transference can also be read as the 'trace' of very present power relations. People experience what they call 'transference' most strongly in hierarchical situations when they are in the junior or subject position, and, of course, ideally, although it does occur in less formal contexts, when they are supine and in a state of vulnerability in relation to another person who is sitting erect, one who is considered an established authority on life, and who denies the subject any information that would situate this authority in his/her lived experience, intentions, or purposes. Here I describe just a few of the conditions and technologies of transference.

Perhaps it would be more appropriate to say that the experience of transference is the trace of power relations that are relatively fixed and approaching a state of domination. So, a strong and ongoing experience of transference can cue people to the fact that they are in a subject position in an inflexible power relationship that could lead to domination. This reading of transference open possibilities for action that can include a refusal of this power relation.

I don't want to be misrepresented on this point. I'm not saying that there is no such phenomenon as transference. And I do understand that there are those who would justify bringing forth this phenomenon with the idea that this establishes a context for working though issues of personal authority, and so on. But I do think that there is a politics associated with this phenomenon, and would raise questions about the deliberate and not so deliberate reproduction of these politics in the therapeutic context. And I would also want to explore the sort of questions that could contribute to a dismantling of the therapeutic structures that reproduce this phenomenon.

Michael H: How would you describe the ethic of your work?

Michael W: To answer this question, we should talk about what is generally meant by ethics. As Foucault (1988a, 1988b) observed, mostly, these days, when people are talking about ethics they are referring to rules and codes, and no doubt these have a place. But it is unfortunate that, in this modern world, considerations of the rule and the code have mostly overshadowed and even replaced considerations of personal ethics. Something precious is lost when institutional codes and rules for the government of conduct supplant notions of personal ethics. It is in the professional disciplines that we see this taken to its limits, and it is done so in the name of assuring appropriate professional conduct.

Invariably, it is argued that the privileging of matters of rule and code is preventative of the exploitation of people who consult therapists. But I don't believe that the elevation of the rule or code has achieved this anywhere the modern world. In fact, it can be argued that such a reliance on the sort of top-down systems of accountability that are associated with systems of rule and code provide fertile ground for the very perpetuation of such injustices, of such exploitation.

At other times, when people are referring to ethics, they are formulating questions about their existence that are informed by what Foucault refers to as a 'will to truth', and, in this modern world, there has been a fantastic incitement to this will to truth. This is a notion of ethics that gives primary consideration to whatever it might be that is understood to constitute expressions of the truth of 'who we are'. The notions of rule and code are central to this version of ethics as well, as whatever it is that constitutes an expression of the truth of who we are is what is informed by the rules of human nature, however nature might be constructed, and however these rules might be determined.

Modern versions of this centre on notions on the rule of needs 'How might we keep faith with our deepest needs?'. It is chilling to consider the sorts of actions that can be justified according to modern need discourses. It is not difficult to apprehend the extent to which this will to truth marginalises considerations of personal ethics, and obscures matters of discourse in the constitution of people's lives. And this will to truth is still about the rule of law, only in this case, it is a 'natural law'.

Then there is another style of ethical consideration that has a long history in western culture, one that is referred to at those times when clashes of interest become apparent between people. This is the sort of consideration that makes it possible for people to discern between actions that are informed by selfishness on the one hand, or by altruism on the other. According to this determination, if altruism can be discerned in the actions in question, then such actions are judged to be ethical. Sarah Hoagland (1988) observes that this style of ethical consideration is one that women have principally been subject to, and that it has played a central role in women's subordination. She powerfully deconstructs this consideration in her book *Lesbian Ethics*.

And other times the criterion of ethical action is not altruism, but 'responsible behaviour' – people can be considered to be behaving ethically when they are taking responsibility in and for their lives. So often, the version of responsibility that is referred to here is one that is informed by the ethic of control. According to this ethic, responsible action is that version of action that reflects independent and singular action on the world that succeeds in bringing about some goal in the relatively short-term, and when these actions are referenced to some universal notion of the good, or some principle, like 'justice' or 'rights'. To behave ethically is to take action that counts in the sense that it 'measures up'. This notion of responsible action that is informed by the ethic of control is the version that Sharon Welch deconstructs in her book *A Feminist Ethic of Risk* (1990).

Michael H: So, what is your account of the ethic of the work we have been discussing?

Michael W: In different places, including during this interview, I have endeavoured to draw out the version of personal ethics that frames the work that I do. I have talked of the knowing formation of the self. I have talked of a version of responsibility which supports a commitment to identifying and addressing the real effects or the consequences of one's actions in the lives of others. And because this is not something that we can independently determine, either by our own interpretations of our immediate experience, or through recourse to some guiding principle, I have talked of the necessity of accountability. This is a specific notion of accountability, a bottom-up version, rather than a top-down version, and it is a version of accountability that is available in partnership with other people, or groups of people. It is an accountability that is in fact constitutive of our lives, one that brings many possibilities for us to become other who we are.

I have also talked of the principle of transparency. This is a principle that is based on a commitment to the ongoing deconstruction of our own actions, of our taken-for-granted ways of being in this work, of our taken-for-granted ways of thinking about life. This is a principle that requires us to situate our opinions, motives and actions in contexts of our ethnicity, class, gender, race, sexual preference, purposes, commitments, and so on.

I have talked of ways of being in the world that have to do with working with others to establish what we could call the 'foundations of possibility' for their lives and for ours. This is not about acting independently on the world to achieve some predicted goal in a proscribed time, but about working collaboratively in the world in taking steps to prepare the foundations for new possibilities in the time that it takes to do this.

And I have talked about many of the other aspects of this ethic, including the extent to which we can make it our business to develop an attitude of reverence for what Malouf calls the little sacraments of daily existence, and the extent to which we can enter into a commitment to challenge the practices and the structures of domination of our culture.

Michael H: So, this ethic suggests a course of action that is distinct from one that is informed by a traditional goal orientation.

Michael W: Yes. It is on the other side of this. But there are important distinctions to be made here. Not all practices that invoke the notion of goal wittingly or unwittingly reproduce this cultures dominant ethic of control. I doubt that anyone would read the work of Steve de Shazer and Insoo Berg in this way.[7] And I also want to state that this is not an argument for a return to long-term therapy. To the contrary. While the ethic of control structures a context in which there are not many events that really count for all that much, this alternative ethic structures a context in which just so much that couldn't be acknowledged previously can be acknowledged. And, in so doing, it provides for an antidote to despair, for a sense of possibility in regard to one's life going forward, and for a broad range of options for further action.

Michael H: Why do you do therapy? Why do you do this work?

Michael W: This is not a new question. Way back in my social work training, which I began in 1967, we were required to address this question. This was in the heyday of structuralist thought. At that time, in response to such questions, only certain accounts of motive were considered acceptable. These were psychological accounts of motive. Accounts of motive that featured notions of conscious purpose and commitment were not fashionable, and were marginalised. Responses to this question that emphasised a wish to contribute to the lives of others in some way, or that were put in terms of a desire to play some part in addressing the injustices of the world, were considered expressions of naivety. Attempts to stand by such expressions were read as examples of denial, lack of insight, bloody-mindedness, etc. On the other hand, to traffick in psychologised accounts of motive was to display insight, truth-saying, a superior level of consciousness, of maturity, and so on. And invariably, the psychologising of motive translated into the pathologising of motive: 'Which of all of one's neurotic needs was being met in stepping into this profession?,'

'How did this decision relate to unresolved issues in one's family of origin?,' 'Did this decision relate to one's attempts to work through an enmeshed relationship with one's mother?', 'Or did this decision relate to one's attempt to work through a disengaged relationship with one's mother?', and so on. I'm sure that you are familiar with questions of this sort, and that we could easily put a list together.

I always believed that this privileging of psychological accounts of motive to be a profoundly conservative endeavour, one that is counter-inspiration, one that could only contribute significantly to therapist experiences of fatigue and burn-out. For various reasons, I could never be persuaded to step into the pathologising of my motives for my interest in joining this profession, and mostly managed to hold onto what were my favoured notions of conscious purpose and commitment. I have no doubt that over the years that expressions of these notions have been a source of invigoration to me, and in recent years have been encouraging therapists to join together in identifying, articulating and elevating notions of conscious purpose and commitment. To this end I have developed an exercise that you can include along with the publication of this transcript. Readers might be interested in meeting with their peers and working through this together. [The exercise immediately follows this interview.]

Michael H: At the beginning of this conference, they showed a short tape that was made two weeks ago of John Weakland greeting the conference, and John invited us to consider what are the priorities in the field now. What is important and what isn't? I wanted to ask if you had a sense of where we're headed, what you think is important, what we need to be doing more of, what you want to privilege?

Michael W: I never want to make a prediction.

Michael H: Not a prediction of where we're going to wind up, but more a sense of ...

Michael W: What's important for us to be looking at?

Michael H: Yeah.

Michael W: It is necessary for us to be taking more seriously what many have been saying about race, culture, gender, ethnicity, class, age, and so on. For too long have we operated with the idea that the people who seek our help have ethnicity and we don't. (Laughter) Not only do we need to join with people in assisting them to locate their experiences in the politics of these contexts, but we are challenged to break from the sort of practices that obscure our own location, and to find ways of engaging with others in reflecting on how this location might be effecting how we interpret our experiences of other people lives, and, of course, how it might be effecting our conduct.

Michael H: I heard Joseph Campbell (1983), when someone asked him his definition of mythology, say it's 'other people's religion', which we kind of dismiss as superstition.

Michael W: Unlike ours. Yeah.

Michael H: Let me read a quotation that gets to something I want to ask. In *Experience, Contradiction, Narrative and Imagination* – a wonderful title as I've come to understand it – you and David Epston (1992, p. 9) comment:

> One of the aspects associated with this work that is of central importance to us is the spirit of adventure. We aim to preserve this spirit and know that if we accomplish this, our work will continue to evolve in ways that are enriching to our lives and to the lives of persons who seek our help.

My question, then, is what's next in your adventure? What's sparking your interest now? I know you began to speak earlier today about some social justice projects.

Michael W: This is a difficult question for me. There are so many things that have my attention at the moment, and they are all things that I want to step more into. Yes, some of these activities do have to do with what are often formally referred to as social justice projects. But this is not a discontinuity. I've always refused the sort of distinctions that put what is commonly referred to as clinical practice in one realm, and community development and social action in another. This is not a distinction that I can relate to. It is a distinction that makes it possible for therapists to treat the therapeutic context as if it is exempt from the relational politics of culture, and to disavow the fact that therapeutic interaction is about action in the world of culture.

Perhaps I can answer your question about 'where to from here' in a different way. I recently saw a movie called *Schindler's List*, and then read a piece about the latter years of Schindler's life. At the time he was living in a bed-sitter somewhere in Southern Germany, I think in Munich. He would frequent the local bars, and on those occasions when he found himself in the company of people of his own generation, he would ask the simple question: 'And what did you do?' – referring, of course, to the Holocaust. Now it was my understanding that this was a genuine question, not a to claim moral superiority. I don't know how many people he found who had answers to this question. I found myself reflecting on this question, and thought it relevant to my life. It is a question that could be asked of me in relation to the many abuses of power and privilege, in relation to the many injustices, that I witness in my immediate world. But if anyone approached to ask this question of me right now, I would request a moratorium on it. I would say, 'Please don't ask me this question yet, it is too soon. I'll keep working on the answer, but please come back later in my life. I hope to have an answer, one that is to my satisfaction, at that time.' And I don't think that it will have to be a big answer, or a grand answer.

Gene: I was just the other day at the Holocaust Museum in Washington. I don't know if you've been there yet, but at the end of the museum you come to a Hall of Remembrance. It's a large open space where there are no flash-cameras or loud noises. And when I got there I sat and found myself making a pledge, to myself or God or whatever ... It wasn't even in specific words, but it was a clear pledge or a promise.

Michael H: I know what you mean. Michael, in Australia, what does 'fair dinkum' mean?

Michael W: It means something said that is absolutely true, deeply genuine.

Michael H: Michael, Gene: 'Fair Dinkum!'

Conscious Purpose and Commitment Exercise

Introduction

We have discussed the extent to which the privileging of psychological accounts of motive has marginalised statements of conscious purpose and commitment in this work. We have reviewed the extent to which such statements are pathologised in the culture of psychotherapy, as well as the implications of this in regard to the stories that we have about who we are as therapists. The following exercise will engage you in acts of resistance to this, acts that are associated with the elevation and reclamation of statements of conscious purpose and commitment. I suggest that you invite another person or two to join you in this exploration, for the purposes of sharing your responses to this exercise, or for the purposes of being interviewed about these responses.

1. Talk about any experiences that you have had that relate to the psychologising and the pathologising of your motives for choosing this work, or any reinterpretations of this choice that may have encouraged you to mistrust your statements of conscious purposes or your personal commitment to this work.

2. Review what you can assume to be some of the real effects or consequences, in your work and your life, of this psychologising of your motives, and of this pathologising of your accounts of your conscious purposes and commitments.

3. Identify and retrieve some of your very early statements of conscious purpose that relate to your chosen work, however unsophisticated these might have been, and reflect on what this suggests about what you are committed to this work.

4. Share some information about the significant experiences of your life that have contributed to a further clarification of your conscious purposes and commitments in taking up this work, that have generated realisations about the particular contribution that you have a determination to make during the course of your life.

5. Discuss the experiences that you are having in the course of this exercise;

those experiences that are associated with engaging in giving testimony, and in bearing witness, to expressions of conscious purpose, those experiences that are associated with the honouring of statements of commitment.

6. Talk about how the elevation of your notions of conscious purpose and the honouring of your statements of commitment could effect:

   a) your experience of yourself in relation to your work,

   b) your relationship to your own life,

   c) your relationship to your colleagues and to the people who seek your help,

   d) the shape of your work and of your life more generally.

Notes

1. As White (1991/1993, p. 34) has written:

   According to my rather loose definition, deconstruction has to do with procedures that subvert taken-for-granted realities and practices: those so-called 'truths' that are split off from the conditions and the context of their production; those disembodied ways of speaking that hide their biases and prejudices; and those familiar practices of self and of relationship that are subjugating of persons' lives. Many of the methods of deconstruction render strange these familiar and everyday taken-for-granted realities and practices by objectifying them.

   He goes on (1991/1993, pp. 35-36) to explain:

   Deconstruction is premised on what is generally referred to as a 'critical constructivist,' or, as I would prefer, a 'constitutionalist' perspective of the world. From this perspective, it is proposed that persons' lives are shaped by the meaning that they ascribe to their experience, by their situation in social structures, and by the language practices and cultural practices of self and of relationship that these lives are recruited into. The narrative metaphor proposes that persons live their lives as stories-that these stories are shaping of life, and that they have real, not imagined, effects-and that these stories provide the structure of life.

2. See Andersen (1991) and Friedman (1995).
3. See Rosenbaum, Hoyt & Talmon (1990).
4. Building on the work of van Gennep (1960) and Turner (1969), White & Epston

(1990); see also Epston & White (1995) suggest that rather than attempting to return a patient in crisis to a 'good enough' status quo, if one thinks of the crisis in terms of a 'rite of passage', then a different construction of the problem is invited; different questions may be asked; and progressive movement is fostered in a different direction. By locating the crisis in relation to a *separation phase,* a liminal or betwixt-and-between phase, and a *reincorporation phase,* the person can determine (1) what the crisis might be telling him or her about separating from what was not viable for him or her, (2) what clues the crisis gives about the new statuses and roles that might become available, and (3) how and under what circumstances the new roles and statuses might be realised.

5. Along related lines, Bruner (1986, p. 153) reminds us of James Joyce's phrase 'epiphanies of the ordinary'. Mary Catherine Bateson's (1995, p. 56) comment is also cogent: 'As a society, we have become so addicted to entertainment that we have buried the capacity for awed experience of the ordinary. Perhaps the sense of the sacred is more threatened by learned patterns of boredom than it is by blasphemies.'

6. See Chapter 16 (pp. 364-365) for Gergen's comments.

7. See Berg (1994), Berg & Miller (1992), Chang & Phillips (1993), de Shazer (1985, 1988, 1991, 1993), and White (1993).

References

Andersen, T. (ed) 1991:*The Reflecting Team: Dialogues and dialogues about the dialogues.* New York: Norton.

Bateson, M.C. 1994: *Peripheral Visions: Learning along the way.* New York: HarperCollins.

Berg, I.K. 1994: *Family Based Services: A solution-focused approach.* New York: Norton.

Berg, I.K. & Miller, S.D. 1992: *Working with the Problem Drinker.* New York: Norton.

Bruner, J. 1986: Actual *Minds, Possible Worlds.* Cambridge, MA: Harvard University Press.

Campbell, J. 1983: *Myths to Live By.* New York: Penguin.

Chang, J. & Phillips, M. 1993: 'Michael White and Steve de Shazer: New directions in family therapy.' In S.G. Gilligan & R. Price (eds), *Therapeutic Conversations* (pp.95-111). New York: Norton.

Combs, G. & Freedman, J. 1990: *Symbol Story, and Ceremony: Using metaphor in individual and family therapy.* New York: Norton.

de Shazer, S. 1985: *Keys to Solutions in Brief Therapy.* New York: Norton.

de Shazer, S. 1988: *Clues: Investigating solutions in brief therapy.* New York: Norton.

de Shazer, S. 1991: *Putting Difference to Work.* New York: Norton.

de Shazer, S. 1993: 'Commentary: de Shazer and White: Vive la difference.' In S.G. Gilligan & R. Price (eds), *Therapeutic Conversations* (pp. 112-120). New York: Norton.

Dulwich Centre Journal (1990-ongoing). (Available from Dulwich Centre Publications, Hutt Street PO Box 7192, Adelaide 5000, Australia)

Epston, D. 1989: *Collected Papers.* Adelaide: Dulwich Centre Publications.

Epston, D. & White, M. 1992: *Experience, Contradiction, Narrative & Imagination: Selected Papers of David Epston and Michael White, 1989-1991.* Adelaide: Dulwich Centre Publications.

Epston, D. & White, M. 1995: 'Termination as a rite of passage: Questioning strategies for a theory of inclusion.' In R.A. Neimeyer & M.J. Mahoney (eds), *Constructivism in Psychotherapy* (pp. 339-354). Washington, DC: American Psychological Association.

Foucault, M. 1988a: 'The ethic of care for the self as a practice of freedom.' In J. Bernauer & D. Rasmussen (eds), *The Final Foucault.* Cambridge, MA: The MIT Press.

Foucault, M. 1988b: 'Technologies of the self.' In L. Martin, H. Gutman & P. Hutton (eds), *Technologies of the Self.* Amherst: University of Massachusetts Press.

Freedman, J. & Combs, G. 1996: *Narrative Therapy: The social construction of preferred realities.* New York: Norton.

Friedman, S. (ed) 1995: *The Reflecting Team in Action: Collaborative practice in family therapy.* New York: Guilford Press.

Geertz, C. 1983: *Local Knowledge.* New York: Basic Books.

Gergen K. 1994: *Between Alienation and Deconstruction: Re-visioning therapeutic communication.* Keynote address, Therapeutic Conversations 2 Conference, Institute for Advanced Clinical Training, Weston, VA.

Gould, S.J. 1980: *The Panda's Thumb: More reflections in natural history.* New York: Norton.

Hoagland, S. 1988: *Lesbian Ethics.* Palo Alto, CA: Institute of Lesbian Studies.

Laing, R.D. 1967: *The Politics of Experience.* New York: Pantheon.

Malouf, D. 1991: *The Great World.* Sydney: Pan MacMillan.

Rosenbaum, R., Hoyt, M.F. & Talmon, M. 1990: 'The challenge of single-session therapies: Creating pivotal moments.' In R.A. Wells & V.J. Giannetti (eds), *Handbook of the Brief Psychotherapies* (pp. 165-189). New York: Plenum Press.

(Reprinted in Hoyt, M.F. [1995], *Brief Therapy and Managed Care: Selected papers* [pp. 105-1391]. San Francisco: Jossey-Bass.)

Suzuki, S. 1970: *Zen Mind, Beginner's* Mind. New York: Weatherhill.

Turner, V. 1969: *The Ritual Process.* Ithaca, NY: Cornell University Press.

van Gennep, A. 1960: *The Rites of Passage.* Chicago: University of Chicago Press.

Welch, S. 1990: *A Feminist Ethic of Risk.* Minneapolis, MN: Fortress Press.

White, M. 1989: *Selected Papers.* Adelaide: Dulwich Centre Publications.

White, M. 1993: 'Deconstruction and therapy.' In S.G. Gilligan & R. Price (eds), *Therapeutic Conversations* (pp. 22-61). New York: Norton. (Original work published in the *Dulwich Centre Newsletter,* 1991, No.3, pp. 1-21. Also reprinted in Epston, D. & White, M. [1992], *Experience, Contradiction, Narrative & Imagination* [pp. 109-152). Adelaide: Dulwich Centre Publications.)

White, M. 1993: 'Commentary. The histories of the present.' In S.G. Gilligan & R. Price (eds), *Therapeutic Conversations* (pp. 121-135). New York: Norton.

White, M. 1994: 'A conversation about accountability with Michael White.' *Dulwich Centre Newsletter,* Nos. 2-3, pp. 68-79. (Reprinted in White, M. [1995], *Re-authoring Lives: Interviews & essays.* Adelaide: Dulwich Centre Publications.)

White, M. 1995: *Re-Authoring lives: Interviews and essays.* Adelaide: Dulwich Centre Publications.

White, M. & Epston, D. 1990: *Narrative Means to Therapeutic* Ends. New York: Norton.

9.

An exploration of aesthetics*

Interviewer: Dave Spellman**

Dave: I will begin by asking you about how you relate to notions of religion and spirituality in your life and in your work.

Michael: I am not religious, although I do acknowledge that I have been born and raised in white Australian culture, which, through its history, has been very significantly shaped by Christianity. So many aspects of Australian ways of life, and so many of the taken-for-granted assumptions associated with these ways of life, wear the hallmarks of Christian culture.

Dave: And what of notions of spirituality?

Michael: About how I relate to spirituality? This notion itself is not one that generally plays itself out in my personal life and in my work in any significant

---

* This interview was first published in *Context: magazine for family therapy and systemic practice*, February 2000, No.47. To subscribe to *Context* please contact Chris Frederick, 12 Mabledon Close, Heald Green, Cheadle, Cheshire SK8 3DB, UK. Ph/fax: (44-161) 493 9012.

** David Spellman is a member of the editorial group of *Context: magazine for family therapy and systemic practice*.

way. However, other therapists have at times reflected on what they consider to be spiritual dimensions of our shared endeavour. I have been interested in their accounts of this, and in their definitions of spirituality. In these conversations I do find some accounts of spirituality that I can join with.

One of these accounts represents a spirituality that is expressed in the knowing action that we take in contributing to the regrading of life. This is a consciousness or, if you like, a spirituality that is expressed in the maintenance of curiosity, in the face of indifference, about what it is that usually passes unnoticed; in attending to what it is that exists in people's lives that is otherwise subject to inattention; and in initiatives taken to rescue the extraordinary from the ordinary. In therapeutic practice, this is a consciousness or a spirituality that contributes to the rich-description of people's lives and identities, one that generates a range of possible actions for them in the knowing formation of their lives and their relationships with others. I do not believe that this is a consciousness or a spirituality that is ever arrived at, but one that requires ongoing efforts to maintain and to further develop (in a culture of unconsciousness).

In responding to this question, I have been thinking of a quote that I recently came across in one of David Malouf's books (1998). I would like to include it here because I believe that it captures well the account of spirituality that I have been discussing:

> *This business of making accessible the richness of the world we are in, of bringing density to ordinary, day-to-day living in a place, is the real work of culture. It is a matter, for the most part, of enriching our consciousness – in both senses of that word: increasing our awareness of what exists around us, making it register on our senses in the most vivid way; but also of taking all that* into *our consciousness and of giving it a second life there so that we possess the world we inhabit imaginatively as well as in fact.* (p. 35)

In reflecting on this quote, I am aware of the extent to which the conversations that I have with the people who consult me contribute to me possessing my own world more imaginatively.

Dave: When I first approached you about the idea of doing this interview, you said something about not being sure you had much to say about the notions of religion and spirituality per se, but that you were interested to say something about the aesthetics surrounding such notions. Could you describe what, for you, constitutes the aesthetics of such notions?

Michael: When we are invited into conversations about spirituality, it is usually, although not always, with the expectation that we will be addressing what is relatively intangible. That is, the expectation is that we will be addressing a phenomenon that is split apart from the material world, one that is manifest on planes above or below the 'surface' of life as it is lived. Although these conversations about spirituality can be very interesting, they are mostly not very revealing of the way that these very notions of spirituality and religion actually shape life.

There are other conversations that can be had that approach particular notions of spirituality and religion as the 'emblems' of particular ways of being in life. It is this consideration that I am more fascinated with. What are the actual life-forming activities that people engage with when their lives are embraced by different notions of spirituality and religion? What are the specific self-forming practices that are associated with these notions? What are the relationship-forming practices that are associated with these notions? What is the style of living that can be discerned as the outcome of these self- and relationship-forming practices? What are the real effects of these styles of living in terms of how one proceeds in life, and in terms of how one contributes to the crafting of the identity of others? And so on.

So, to explore the aesthetics of spiritual and religious notions contributes to the unpacking of these notions in ways that provide us with an appreciation of what I would call their material aspects. Apart from all else, this unpacking presents the opportunity for us to attend to the consequences of how we live our lives.

Dave: How did you come to make such a distinction, i.e. the aesthetics of such notions from the notions themselves?

Michael: I have always found the poststructuralist sentiment to be the more engaging sentiment. This sentiment is expressed in questions like: 'Through these acts of living, through these expressions of life, in what ways are we becoming other than who we were?'; 'How might these options for action in the world, for our expressions of life, contribute to us becoming other than who we are at this present time?'. I find these to be more interesting and exciting questions than those shaped by the structuralist sentiment: 'What is the truth of our human nature/spirituality?'; 'How might this truth be revealed?'.

Poststructuralist questions are those that draw our attention to the constituted nature of identity. Questions like these, and others, bring our attention to considerations of aesthetics.

Dave: I suppose this interest in what you are calling a poststructuralist sentiment and the aesthetics of religion and spirituality have been reinforced by some of the possibilities that this brings to your practice. Has it also been supported by your reading? If so, what are your sources?

Michael: Yes. This interest has been supported by my reading of a number of authors. Perhaps I could mention Michel Foucault here, as many of your readers would know that I have a longstanding engagement with his ideas. A specific focus of Foucault's work was the history of the fabrication of the human subject, with an emphasis on the constitution of the self as a moral agent. In this endeavour he inquired into the elaboration of one's relationship to oneself through different eras, and referred to this as the study of ethics.

In these studies, Foucault concluded that, through different eras, there could be identified four aspects in the constitution of self as a moral agent. He called the first aspect of the constitution of the self as a moral agent the 'ethical substance'. The ethical substance is that aspect of life that is considered of primary relevance to ethical judgement. This ethical substance is whatever it is about our lives that is our responsibility to manage well, and this includes what is often referred to as concupiscence. These ethical substances could be the pleasures, the desires, motives, needs, personal properties, attributes, and so on.

The second aspect of the constitution of the self as a moral agent is the 'mode of subjectification'. It is the mode of subjectification which provides the mechanism through which people are encouraged or required to recognise their moral obligations in regard to the management of the relevant ethical substances. For example, in the judgement of one's management of the relevant

An exploration of aesthetics

ethical substances, is one to refer to divine laws, to the laws of nature, to rational rule, to particular systems of values and principles, for example, like the system of values that is expressed in certain religious or humanist narratives, and so on?

The third aspect of the constitution of self as a moral agent is what Foucault referred to as 'asceticism', and he gave this term a broad definition. Asceticism is about the self-forming activities that one engages in when observing the obligations that one has to become an ethical subject in the pursuit of an ethical existence. These self-forming activities include techniques of the self, which also implicate practices in the formation of relationships with others, and with communities of people. These activities might be what one does to moderate one's pleasures, to decipher and to modulate one's desires, to police one's motives, to discipline one's thoughts, to regulate one's needs, to cultivate one's properties, and so on.

The fourth aspect of the constitution of self as a moral agent is 'telos'. Telos is about the mode of being or the kind of being that we aspire to be when we are behaving in a moral way. Telos expresses the goal or the end point in one's identity project. For example, it might be an aspiration to achieve a life that is one of purity, of godliness, of personal fulfilment or liberation, or of a life that is a work of art.

Dave: So how do these considerations of Foucault contribute to your appreciation of the aesthetics of religious or spiritual notions?

Michael: Considerations such as these contribute to the possibilities for conversations that are unpacking of spiritual and religious notions. For example, in conversations with people about their spiritual and religious notions, I can ask a whole range of questions about what it is that they have a responsibility to manage well in their lives (ethical substance), what it is that they are observing in this management, and in their judgements about the success of these efforts (mode of subjectification), the self- and relationship-shaping activities that they engage in through the pursuit of an ethical existence (asceticism), and to what they are aspiring to become through the moral development of their life (telos).

This unpacking contributes to possibilities for me to appreciate the proposals for life, the practices and the skills of living, and the styles of existence that are associated with a range of spiritual and religious notions. These knowledges and skills usually turn out to be highly relevant to addressing the various predicaments, problems, dilemmas and concerns for which people seek therapy. It is through this unpacking that I find many spiritual and religious notions to be quite beautiful. And it is through this unpacking that spiritual and religious notions can be separated from the institutionalised politics of religion.

Dave: Have you ever worked with religious men and women or seen people who hold some strong religious beliefs? Would you ask about such things, and is the work different from the rest of your work?

Michael: Yes, I do see men and women who hold strong religious beliefs. And I do ask about such things. In these circumstances we can have extended conversations about all of these elements. For example, in conversations about what Foucault calls 'mode of subjectification', we can review how it is that one engages with, say, 'divine law' or 'God's word', and how one is applying oneself to this, which is very much one's own business, not just God's. By this I mean that in this review people have the opportunity to identify some of the self-shaping activities that they engage in with regard to the construction of their own lives and identities.

I would say that these conversations invariably contribute to an appreciation of, or a multiplication of, complexity in regard to spiritual and religious notions, to a greater range of possible actions in achieving whatever it is that is being aspired to, or to possibilities that, in the context of therapy, would not otherwise have been considered for addressing certain predicaments. And, when consulted, those who are living in close relationships with these persons who have strong religious beliefs are usually quite clear about which of these possibilities are preferred over others.

Dave: Is this what Foucault did?

Michael: No. Foucault had other purposes in studying the history of the constitution of self as a moral agent. One of these was to demonstrate that the modes of life and thought associated with modern identities are not any more the product of the 'givens' of human nature than historical modes of life and thought, despite the assertions of modern scientific rationality. Another purpose was to support his assertion that we do not have to be tied to the unquestioned reproduction of the cherished individualities of contemporary western culture. He hoped to achieve this, in part, by drawing out, in history, the continuities and discontinuities in the constitution of identity in ways that demonstrate that things have not always been as they are and, therefore, do not have to be as they are. A third factor was Foucault's desire for the development of a more experimental culture, one that was more embracing of options for constituting life according to a range of aesthetic considerations.

But I have found these ideas to be very useful in joining with people in the unpacking or deconstruction of spiritual and religious notions. These ideas have provided a basis for therapeutic inquiry that contributes to the rich description of the ways of life and thought that are associated with these notions. However, in referring here to these ideas of Foucault, I don't want to imply that these provide the most useful basis for this sort of therapeutic inquiry, or that this analysis is relevant to all notions of spirituality. There are many other analyses that can equally contribute to this sort of deconstruction of spiritual and religious notions.

Dave: You have an interesting take on deconstruction. There have been concerns voiced that if we unpack or deconstruct everything, then we will have nothing left. What are your thoughts about this?

Michael: I have also seen such conclusions in some of the literature, and I am curious about them. It is my understanding that the unpacking or deconstruction of identity categories, regardless of what these are (religious or otherwise), contributes very significantly to an appreciation of complexity of these categories, and to the rich description of the knowledges and skills of living that are associated with them. Reduction is never an outcome of this sort of unpacking or deconstruction. Rather, it is through this deconstruction that complexity is apprehended. And it is in the apprehension of this complexity that more options for action in the world become available to the people who consult us.

In these conversations that deconstruct religious or spiritual notions, people do not experience any disrespect of what it is that they hold sacred, or any dismantling of treasured experiences. Rather, the rich description of knowledges and skills of living, and the apprehension of complexity, that is an outcome of these conversations, is usually experienced to be honouring of religious and spiritual notions.

Dave: Do you know of other therapists who have a similar understanding of deconstruction and who take this up with people in conversations about religion and spirituality?

Michael: Yes. In some religious traditions can be found the idea of engaging in conversations with God for the purposes of clarifying spiritual directions and for addressing the predicaments of one's life. These traditions often specify the actual practices for achieving this. There are therapists who have taken this idea, and these practices, into therapeutic contexts, and who have there joined with people in applying this tradition to therapeutic objectives. It is in these explorations of people's conversations with God that many spiritual and religious notions are deconstructed. This is a deconstruction that contributes to the sort of options that I have been referring to in this interview. Those therapists who come most immediately to mind, in regard to this work, are Melissa Griffith and James Griffith, of Washington DC. And, in the pages of this issue of Context, David Harper gives some account of such conversations.

Dave: Many people I have spoken to acknowledge a 'spirit' of your work they do not see much elsewhere. I understand this to relate to the much broader canvass you paint on and notions of community you have developed as well as the enthusiasm and personal voice with which you speak. Does this description make sense to you? Is a 'spirit' important in your ideas about your work? Is 'spirituality' in some form important?

Michael: This description does make sense to me, but, although I do appreciate this acknowledgement, I am too centred in this description for my comfort. I take this use of the word 'spirit' to here refer to 'ethos', and while I am prepared to acknowledge the contribution that I make to this, I am keenly aware of the extent to which this ethos is shaped by the sentiments that people bring with them into these circles. These people usually step into these circles with a degree of goodwill and benevolence towards us as therapists and community workers, with an intention to find ways to join with us so that we might together have some good conversations about what is important to them. They persevere with us and usually express a good deal of patience when we get off track. They often express compassion in their understandings of how hard pressed we are at times, and are frequently gracious in bringing us down to earth when, in our suggestions, we confuse our lives with theirs.

I think that, as therapists and community workers, one part that we can play in the development of this ethos is to take the time to identify and to acknowledge the contributions of this sort that are made by the people who seek our consultation or assistance.

Dave: Some have described you as a charismatic family therapy guru and those who attend workshops as 'disciples' and I don't think they mean that in a good way! What would you say about that?

Michael: The charisma thing I don't relate to. I am regularly involved in teaching contexts in Australia and abroad, and this has provided me with the time and the opportunity to explore teaching styles that make it more possible for me to achieve a joining with the people who attend my workshops, and that hopefully make the ideas and practices of narrative therapy accessible, including those ideas and practices that relate to the more complex cultural and historical considerations of identity. However, there have been occasions upon which I have not been particularly effective in this, and on these occasions my identity has been described in other ways which I don't care to relate here!

As for 'disciples', 'followers', 'converts', 'devotees' and so on, I have heard these descriptions and have seen them in writing. I agree with you that the tenor of these descriptions is negative. They negatively construct the people who attend these workshops, and negatively construct my purposes. These descriptions take the form of a denouncement. Perhaps this is, in part, an outcome of the blurring of distinctions around denouncement and critique. I don't believe that anything should go unquestioned. I would feel highly uncomfortable if anything that I say, write or do, that has the potential to influence others, was to be considered exempt from being questioned. Regardless of the possibilities that are associated with any idea or practice, there are also limitations and possible hazards, some of which can be identified through critique. I welcome this, even though at times it has been difficult for me when I have been challenged on actions that have reproduced the very subjugating effects that I am consciously opposed to. But these are conversations that I want to stay in, or at least come back to after some reflection.

But I do not perceive an invitation to conversation in these denouncements, and in the misrepresentations of what I have said and written that is usually associated with them. I have no wish to engage in conversation under these circumstances. And conversation under these circumstances is made doubly difficult because, in these denouncements of me and the people who attend my workshops, descriptions that have a special and treasured meaning for those of different religious persuasions (i.e. disciples, followers, converts, devotees) are being used in a derogatory sense. At times I have found raising my concerns about this difficult going, for, in addressing these, I have been accused of being 'politically correct', when it is my understanding that I am honouring some learnings about the negative effects of the use of descriptions that have treasured, and, at times, sacred meanings to others. These are learnings that have been offered to me by people who have been prepared to speak of their experience of the employment of these meanings in ways that are degrading of them.

So, I do not believe that these efforts to address the use of language have anything to do with political correctness. Rather, these efforts have to do with being available to some understanding of what it means to others when terms are used this way, and to make a decision about whether to continue to use these terms in this way or to find other terms of description that are adequate for the task at hand and that do not have these untoward effects.

Dave: In the same vein, how would you respond to accusations that there is a religiosity to your work?

Michael: Again, I think that this is often about denouncement, but, on any account, I find this conclusion astounding. Narrative therapy, as I understand it, is not associated with some global proposal about how things should be. Rather, it is about local inquiry into what is happening, into how things are becoming other than what they were, or into the potential for things to become other than what they are. The skills of narrative practice provide a context for the rich description of the knowledges and skills of living expressed in all of this, and for the exploration of the possibilities, limitations and possible hazards associated with how things are and with how things are becoming other than what they were.

If these comments about religiosity are intended to establish claims about parallels between the proposals and practices of narrative therapy and religious principles and practices, then I believe these comments to be trivialising of the very significant achievements that are represented in religious developments. I do not believe that it is possible, in the ideas and practices of what is referred to as narrative therapy, to find any unified or, for that matter, any even limited agreement about adequate responses to the questions that we were discussing earlier in this interview – those questions about relevant ethical substance, about mode of subjectification, about asceticism, and about telos. But more than this, even if some limited agreement could be achieved, whatever it was that there was agreement around could not be ascribed any special 'truth' status. For it would be quickly deconstructed by locating it in history and culture.

Dave: Our time is nearly up and we are coming to the end of this interview. Is there anything that we haven't covered that you would have particularly liked to have taken up here?

Michael: Perhaps it would have been good to talk a little about the sense of being in community with others that is a significant outcome of our practice. By this I mean the sense that is the outcome of experiencing some of the stories of our lives joined with the stories of the lives of others around shared themes and values. Not only does this make it possible for us to appreciate aspects of our lives and relationships that might not otherwise be visible to us, but it also contributes to us developing more multi-voiced lives. In experiencing other people's voices with us in this way, we find that we are less condemned to the single-voiced identities that are the vogue of contemporary western culture. I refer to this, as, although I do not have a metaphysical understanding of this, some people do read this sense of being within community in the material absence of that community as something spiritual.

And while we are talking about sense of community, I would like to say how much I have enjoyed getting together with you on this project. It has been quite some years since you visited Adelaide, but during this interview I have had quite vivid memories of our conversations of that time.

Reference

Malouf, D. 1998: *A Spirit of Play: The making of Australian consciousness*. Sydney: ABC Books.

What is narrative therapy?

An easy-to-read introduction

by
Alice Morgan

What is narrative therapy? This easy-to-read introduction seeks to answer this question through the use of accessible language, a concise structure and a wide range of practical examples. This book covers a broad spectrum of narrative practices including externalisation, re-membering, therapeutic letter writing, the use of rituals, leagues, reflecting teams and much more. It contains an easy to use index to assist readers in looking up any ideas that they may be particularly interested in. Suggestions for further reading are also listed throughout. If you are a therapist, health worker or community worker who is trying to, or is wanting to apply narrative ideas in your own work context, this book has been written with you in mind!

published by, and available from:

Dulwich Centre Publications
Hutt St PO Box 7192
Adelaide, South Australia 5000
phone (61-8) 8223 3966 fax (61-8) 8232 4441
email: dcp@senet.com.au
www.dulwichcentre.com.au

2001

February 14th-16th
Adelaide, Australia

International narrative therapy & community work conference

Timed to coincide with the acclaimed world music festival WOMADelaide, this diverse event will feature formal workshops, keynote addresses, practice-based seminars, tent sessions, discussions 'under the trees' and much more. Some of the most thoughtful presenters of narrative ideas and ways of working will come together in a festival-like atmosphere. Workshops and other events will surround the conference to enable participants to make the most of their time in Adelaide (including a women's gathering and book fair).

Speakers confirmed include: David Epston, Kathy Weingarten, Stephen Madigan, Ann Hartman, Michael White, Jill Freedman, Gene Combs, Maggie Carey, Joan Laird, Alice Morgan, The Anti-Harassment Team, Yael Gershoni, Saviona Cramer, The Family Centre (Lower Hutt) and many more ...

For more information please contact us!

Phone: 61 8 8223 3966
Fax: 61 8 8232 4441
Email: dulwich@senet.com.au
Homepage: www.dulwichcentre.com.au

Narrative therapy and community work:
A conference collection

This book represents a range of workshops, presentations and conversations that took place at the inaugural Dulwich Centre Publications' Narrative Therapy and Community Work Conference in Adelaide in February 1999. From practice-based seminar papers, to the perspectives of Indigenous Australia, to hearing from the voices of young people, this collection contains a diversity of thoughtful and invigorating writings. Contributors include writers from Israel, Australia, New Zealand, North America and South Africa.

published by, and available from:

Dulwich Centre Publications
Hutt St PO Box 7192
Adelaide, South Australia 5000
phone (61-8) 8223 3966 fax (61-8) 8232 4441
email: dcp@senet.com.au
www.dulwichcentre.com.au

Extending Narrative Therapy:
A collection of practice-based papers

We are pleased to announce a new book which consists of a collection of papers that have been published by Dulwich Centre Publications in the last few years, all of which take the practices of narrative therapy into new territories.

These papers extend on possibilities in relation to externalising conversations, group work, and community work. Other sections include 'In our own voice', in which authors write of the ways they have re-authored aspects of their own experience: 'Talking about sexual abuse' and 'New ways of introducing narrative therapy'.

This book has been put together for practitioners who wish to keep in touch with the latest ways in which people are extending narrative ideas in their own contexts.

published by, and available from:

Dulwich Centre Publications
Hutt St PO Box 7192
Adelaide, South Australia 5000
phone (61-8) 8223 3966 fax (61-8) 8232 4441
email: dcp@senet.com.au
www.dulwichcentre.com.au

www.ingramcontent.com/pod-product-compliance
Lightning Source LLC
Chambersburg PA
CBHW070659100426
42735CB00039B/2322